THE MIRACULOUS MEDAL

THE
MIRACULOUS
MEDAL

Stories, Prayers, and Devotions

Donna-Marie Cooper O'Boyle

franciscan
media
Cincinnati, Ohio

Cover design by Candle Light Studios
Cover image © Shutterstock
Book design by Mark Sullivan

LIBRARY OF CONGRESS CATALOGING-IN-PUBLICATION DATA
O'Boyle, Donna-Marie Cooper.
The miraculous medal : stories, prayers, and devotions / Donna-Marie Cooper O'Boyle.
pages cm
Summary: "Over twenty years ago, Mother Teresa gave Donna-Marie Cooper O'Boyle a blessed Miraculous Medal, and she has never taken it off. To date, Donna-Marie has given away thousands of Miraculous Medals. But what is the Miraculous Medal—and why is it considered miraculous? Why is it important for us today? You'll learn the answers to these questions, and you'll also discover: The origin and history of the Miraculous Medal, How the medal got its name, The story of St. Catherine Laboure. The author has collected many contemporary stories of the Miraculous Medal's attraction and impact. Also provided is a section of prayers and devotions, including the perpetual novena prayer, spiritual benefits, and more. This is an informative, fascinating, and inspiring book, designed to stir the hearts of those who aren't familiar with the Miraculous Medal's miraculous powers through the Blessed Mother's intercession, as well as those who are— Provided by publisher.
Includes bibliographical references and index.
ISBN 978-1-61636-625-4 (pbk.)
1. Miraculous Medal. I. Title.
BX2163.5.O26 2013
242'.74—dc23
2013015724
ISBN 978-1-61636-625-4

Published by Franciscan Media
28 W. Liberty St.
Cincinnati, OH 45202
www.FranciscanMedia.org

To the Mother of God, Queen of Heaven and Earth, compassionate Mother of all mankind, may this book attract souls to your Immaculate Heart!

For all of my children: Justin, Chaldea, Jessica, Joseph, and Mary-Catherine, may you always seek grace and guidance from Mother Mary.

O Mary, conceived without sin, pray for us who have recourse to thee!

[C O N T E N T S]

[I N T R O D U C T I O N]

As I begin to write *The Miraculous Medal: Stories, Prayers, and Devotions*, which tells the story of the Blessed Mother working through her Miraculous Medal, my heart is brimming with gratitude and bursting with the stories I'd like to share with you. My aim is to draw your attention to Our Lady of the Miraculous Medal, and I hope, by God's grace and the Blessed Mother's intercession, to rekindle an exceptional devotion to it among all Catholics and Christians.

Growing up in a large Catholic family, I was forever seeing Miraculous Medals throughout my life. My mother's petite, delicate, blue Miraculous Medal hung from her golden watchband. It's now tucked away safely in my jewelry box atop my bureau. She also wore a Miraculous Medal around her neck. My grandmother Alexandra Uzwiak wore a Miraculous Medal, too. At times when my mother and grandmother were engrossed in a deep conversation (speaking in Polish), my grandmother naturally fingered her Miraculous Medal, now and then rubbing it with more passion when the conversation turned to serious matters.

My godmother, Aunt Bertha, kept her medal pinned securely to her clothing, close to her heart. I'm sure that some of my other numerous aunts, uncles, and cousins wore the medal also, for I have fond memories of times when we gathered together for picnics and family gatherings and I could see a glimmering of the silver or gold medals around their necks. I remember that the religious sisters who taught me at St. Mary's school wore Miraculous Medals as well.

Throughout my childhood years I wore a Miraculous Medal, as did some of my brothers and sisters. We often received one as a gift at our baptism, first Holy Communion, or confirmation. We were Catholic, after all. The medals came with the territory.

I would later be blessed to receive Miraculous Medals from Mother Teresa. It wasn't until still later on in my life that I really thought about the Miraculous Medal and what it truly means to wear one. That's precisely what I want to share with you in this book.

I think it is wonderful and wise of the Church to offer sacramentals, faithful holy reminders, to make our faith more tangible—more *real*, if I may say so. Wearing our Miraculous Medal is a holy reminder of a God who loves us immensely and who wants us to live eternally with him in heaven one day. This same God even gave us his Mother as he hung from the cross.

Yesterday, November 27, was the anniversary of the day that the Blessed Mother visited Sister Catherine Labouré in the motherhouse in Paris, giving her instructions to have the Miraculous Medals made. It was during an era of great unrest, revolution, and wars, and a prevailing hopelessness was settling on France. Many had lost their faith or had stopped practicing it. The Blessed Mother told Sister Catherine, "The times are very evil." Subsequently, the Miraculous Medal brought many promised graces, and a spiritual renewal flourished throughout Europe and the world.

We live in "very evil" times as well. Countless people have lost their faith or are not practicing it. On this feast of St. Catherine Labouré, November 28, I pray that—by means of God's grace, the intercession of Our Lady of the Miraculous Medal, and the intercession of St. Catherine Labouré—in telling St. Catherine Labouré's story as well as recounting modern-day occurrences of the spiritual effects and benefits of the Miraculous Medal—that each person who reads this book will be deeply inspired and blessed. Additionally, because of the Blessed Virgin's intercession, I pray that the floodgates of an astounding spiritual renewal will be opened throughout the world.

O Mary, conceived without sin, pray for us who have recourse to thee! *Totus Tuus!*

> *Donna-Marie Cooper O'Boyle*
> *November 28, 2012*
> *Feast of St. Catherine Labouré*

St. Catherine Labouré, Model of Humility

"I knew nothing; I was nothing. For this reason God picked me out."[1]
—St. Catherine Labouré

St. Catherine Labouré was born to pious parents, Pierre and Madeleine Louise Labouré, at the ringing of the *Angelus* bell at 6:00 PM on May 2, 1806, in the serene and charming village of Fain-lès-Moutiers in the Burgundy region of France. No sooner had Catherine been born and drawn up close to her mother's breast that Madeleine Louise requested that her daughter's name be entered immediately on the civil register. Because of her mother's earnest plea, due perhaps to a holy intuition, within a quarter of an hour after her birth Catherine was registered: "Catherine, daughter of Pierre Labouré and Madeleine Gontard his wife, was born this same day (May 2, 1806) at six o'clock in the evening."[2] It turns out that Catherine was the only one of their seventeen children that would be registered so quickly. In addition, her name was registered with the church the very next day on the feast of the Finding of the Cross, when Catherine was baptized into the Catholic Church.

Perhaps only our Lord and his Blessed Mother knew of the holy significance in Catherine coming into this world at the sounding of Mary's bells for the *Angelus*, the prayer commemorating the angel Gabriel's announcement to the Blessed Mother that she conceived of the Holy Spirit. It would be many years before one might have reason to ponder the connection—the saint who would herald in the Marian age was graced with the ringing of the *Angelus* bells from every church and chapel around at the first moment of her life on earth. The memorial of the Finding of the Cross on Catherine's baptismal day would also prove to be significant to her life as she became devoted to the holy cross and one day would even experience a mystical vision of it.

The Labouré family rarely used Catherine's baptismal name. Instead, Catherine was affectionately referred to as Zoe, possibly after an obscure local saint on whose feast she was born. Zoe was so much a part of Catherine's identity that one time she signed her name "Catherine Labouré Zoe" on a baptismal registry when she served as godmother to a neighbor's child.

Catherine grew up in her close-knit family on a farm in the quaint little village of Fain, comprised of barely a hundred and fifty inhabitants. Catherine's father, Pierre, who had entered the seminary in his teens but gave up the notion of becoming a priest to instead take up farming, ruled the household and farm with a somewhat iron hand. Catherine's mother, Madeleine Louise, a former teacher from a cultured background, made up for Pierre's gruffness and lack of warmth. She was gentle and saintly. Both were educated, and both were committed to raising saintly children.

The Labouré family lived comfortably in their spacious house on a picturesque farm. They enjoyed the simple comfort of having enough but didn't give in to wastefulness or luxuries. A servant helped the busy Madeleine with some of the household chores and care of the many children. Of the seventeen children that Madeleine bore, only eleven survived. Six babies died at birth, and one, Alexandre, died at age one. Her son Auguste was permanently disabled in an unfortunate accident when the family's horse-drawn buggy overturned during what should have been a happy family outing; from that day on he needed constant care, adding to Madeleine's many responsibilities.

Pierre labored from early morning until sundown, not afraid to get his hands dirty, while overseeing a dozen farmhands and managing the bountiful property. He tilled the soil, produced grains, and he also raised pigeons for market, which is a native French industry. By ancient law Pierre was one of the few farmers in his area given permission to maintain the trade. Town folks were familiar with the sight of hundreds of pigeons flying in and out of the stone dovecote on the Labouré farm. The sound of their wings flapping almost in unison probably startled many an unsuspecting bystander. Catherine, when she was old enough to help, delighted in caring for the pigeons, which would swoop down impatiently when she entered the dwelling with their feed, sometimes mussing her hair.

Catherine followed her mother around the house as she went about her chores. Her little sister Tonine toddled behind her, both girls learning from their mother and becoming familiar with the housekeeping with which they would later help. The seven older brothers helped in the household until they were old enough to go out into the fields with their father.

Catherine's older sister, Marie Louise, was taken in by Madeleine Louise's sister and husband who lived in Langres. She was raised by the childless couple as if she were their own and educated by the Sisters of Charity in Langres. Though it was heroic and noble of them, Pierre and Madeleine must have experienced great pain in giving up their daughter even if it was to deserving relatives.

A larger life existed outside of the quaint village of rolling fields and demanding farm life. Two of the older sons left home: The oldest son, Hubert, went off to the army, and Jacques left for Paris to work in a business firm. Soon after, Antoine left for Paris, too, pursuing work as a pharmacist's apprentice. The nest was getting a bit smaller, and Madeleine was keeping her daughters Catherine and Tonine close. She didn't send them to school when they were old enough, apparently wanting to cling to them for as long as she could. Of course, Auguste was always nearby as well.

Little Catherine and her mother remained close to each other, bonded in a spiritual sense as well, until October 9, 1815, when Catherine's mother shut her eyes on her earthly life. God called her home when she was only forty-two years old. Suddenly, the Labouré family had to grapple with the fact that the heart of their home had died.

Catherine felt utterly lost. Mama was gone—forever. Everyone felt the immense absence and knew that life would never be the same. Charles went off to Paris to be trained in the restaurant business, and Joseph and Pierre went off to boarding school. Marie Louise came back home to help. She was twenty years old now. She and the servant (who eventually merited the affectionate title of "Mama") would care for Catherine, who was now nine, Tonine, who was seven, and Auguste, who was six.

Choosing Mary

Watching a mother's burial is no easy feat for anyone, never mind a little girl, but Catherine managed to get through it by means of quiet tears and many prayers. A few days later, Catherine wandered into her parents' bedroom and gazed up at the statue of the Blessed Mother set high up on a shelf. She looked over her shoulder to see if anyone was nearby, and since she was alone, she confidently pushed a chair closer to the shelf and got up on it. Reaching up, she took down the statue and hugged it close to her heart. She spoke earnestly and directly to the Mother of God: "Now, dear Blessed Mother, now you will be my Mother!"

Just like that, Catherine expressed her desires and with a childlike confidence thoroughly expected that Mary would indeed listen, come to her aid, and be her Mother. We are certain about this intended secret display of Catherine's affection toward Mother Mary because unbeknownst to her, providentially, a household servant was surreptitiously watching. Catherine was so caught up in the spiritual experience that she hadn't heard the servant come up quietly from behind.

A few centuries before, St. Teresa of Avila also chose Mary for her Mother while praying before a statue of Mary when her mother died. Nine-year-old Catherine wouldn't have known about St. Teresa's pronouncement, but we know she was certainly in good company in her decision.

At this time, Pierre's sister, Marguerite, and her husband, Antoine Jeanrot, offered to take Catherine and Tonine into their family for a time to help ease the load on Marie Louise and the servant, who was responsible for caring for the kids and household and for feeding the dozen farmhands. The girls would have playmates—four girls, their older cousins who could dote over them. So, it was decided that they would go to the Jeanrot home in the beautiful town of Saint-Rémy.

Colorful gardens walled in stone rolled over the property, while picturesque views of a heavenly countryside painted a striking backdrop. Christian values prevailed in the pleasant atmosphere of the new home setting. The girls missed their family back in Fain but enjoyed being smothered in love and compassion by their kind relatives.

Catherine was different from children her age and even children older than her. Her mother had seen this in her: Catherine reached for heavenly things. She was growing in holiness and clandestinely desiring that she might someday see the Blessed Mother. She was absolutely delighted that Saint-Rémy possessed a resident priest, which meant many more opportunities to attend church services. Catherine's desire for holy things was edifying.

In fact, her eighteen-year-old cousin, Claudine, was taken aback to see Catherine's attention at church, her hands folded devotedly while kneeling up nice and straight. Claudine not only admired her younger cousin's devotion, but she began to grow in holiness herself by imitating Catherine's devoutness. The whole Jeanrot family grew in their faith because of a little girl's piety.

Weeks grew into months, and unexpectedly the intended short stay at the relatives' home became a stay of two years. Within that time, the Jeanrots' vinegar business continued to excel to such a degree that Marguerite became stretched in keeping up with helping her husband run the business and caring for the younger visiting relatives. Something else was brewing, too. Catherine's older sister, Marie Louise, felt a calling to the Daughters of Charity, the sisters who had taught her throughout her life. Her duties caring for the household in Fain after her mother died had caused her previous dreams of her vocation to be put on hold. Now twenty-two years old, Mary Louise desired to enter the religious life more than ever. These two situations made the decision for the girls to return home to their father the most sensible solution.

Catherine was twelve years old at the time but very mature for her age. She was entrusted with the care of the household by her father, which meant she would, along with the servant, cook and clean; care for Tonine, Auguste, and her brothers when they were home from boarding school; and provide meals for the hired hands as well. Catherine didn't mind this in the least. She was happy that she could release the chains that prevented Marie Louise from pursuing the convent.

Receiving Jesus

Just a few weeks after returning home to her father's house, on January 25, 1818, the feast of the Conversion of St. Paul, Catherine received Jesus for the first time during her first Holy Communion. From that day onward, Catherine continued to grow in holiness and longed for Jesus more and more intensely. She began to attend Mass each morning and to receive Holy Communion frequently. To do so, she had to walk a good distance to a neighboring parish very early in the morning, since her own parish in Fain did not provide a daily Mass. At that time, daily Communion was not allowed (until about a hundred years later), but Catherine received her Lord in Communion whenever she was allowed to do so.

Catherine scheduled prayer times into her busy days, which were already heaped with chores. She even began fasting on Fridays and Saturdays. She rarely partook in normal childlike pastimes and possessed a maturity beyond her years in recognizing the importance in taking breaks for prayer, in order to connect with God whenever she could. In between her chores and duties, Catherine would slip away to a secluded corner somewhere in the spacious Labouré farmhouse to pray silently for even a few moments. At times, her little sister Tonine would find her and observe the mystical glow on Catherine's face.

One of the wonderful things about being back in Fain was the old village church, which had been there for centuries. It was right across the lane, barely a few steps away from her home. If she had a little time between chores, she could skip over, slip inside, and enjoy a respite of prayer with God, Mary, the angels, and the saints. Sometimes she would kneel, and other times she would walk the Stations of the Cross, a prayer she loved.

Partly because Catherine's father presided as the mayor of Fain for a time, and also because the family donated substantially to the parish to help with repairs, the villagers found it fitting to gift the family with a chapel in their name, for their use alone: the Labouré chapel. Besides the old village church, it was here in the holy setting of the Labouré chapel, her private shrine, that Catherine could commune with God alone. The painting of the Annunciation that graced the chapel wall was a constant reminder to Catherine of the momentous encounter of the Blessed Mother and the angel Gabriel. How interesting that Catherine should see this sight day after day, year after year—the girl who was born at the ringing of the *Angelus* bells.

Her Transfixing Dream

One night, when Catherine was eighteen, she had an unforgettable dream. She was in the Labouré chapel assisting at a Mass of an elderly priest. She had never seen him before. He kept looking into her eyes each time he turned from the altar for the *"Dominus vobiscum."* Every time, Catherine looked down because it startled her. After Mass, the old priest asked Catherine to follow him to the sacristy, but Catherine bolted from the church and ran home. Looking over her shoulder once, she saw that the priest was still watching her from the door. Next in the dream, Catherine decided to visit a sick woman. When she entered her room she almost walked right into the same priest! She tried to get away, but the priest looked straight at her and spoke to her: "You do well to visit the sick, my child. You flee from me now, but one day you will be glad to come to me. God has plans for you; do not forget it."

Catherine woke up and instantly wondered what her dream could possibly have meant. She knew that trying to interpret dreams was tricky business and not something humans were necessarily meant to do. But this dream was so vivid, so real, so haunting. Even so, Catherine felt a sudden sense of peace and happiness filling her heart. She didn't know then what her strange dream proposed, but she would understand it later on. Catherine didn't reveal the dream to anyone until about four years later when it came out in a conversation with her confessor. She didn't mention it again until close to the end of her life.

During the next few years, Catherine received at least three marriage proposals. She turned each one down politely. She had made a promise to Jesus to become a consecrated religious, and she was committed to keeping it. Catherine's father was happy each time an interested suitor was turned down, pleased that she would be home with him a bit longer.

At twenty-two years old, Catherine confidently believed she had faithfully served her father by caring for the family and household. It was now time for her to follow her vocation. Tonine was now twenty years old and would be able to take her place. Catherine had a long heart-to-heart talk with Tonine, and Tonine was up to the task and supportive of Catherine's goals. Catherine prayed for the right timing to discuss her plan with her father. Though Pierre knew his daughter was extraordinarily kind and pious, he didn't yet grasp the reality of Catherine's religious calling.

Much to Catherine's surprise and disappointment, her father flat out said, "No!" That was it. He was not about to let another daughter leave him for religious life—no further discussion. We can imagine Catherine's frustration and sadness.

Paris Was Beckoning

Right at that time, Catherine's brother Charles, who had opened his own restaurant after learning the trade in Paris, wrote to his father. In the letter he mentioned that he needed domestic help, mostly because his wife had died prematurely not long before. Pierre immediately thought of sending Catherine to help since there had been some tension between them because of his negativity toward Catherine's desire to become a religious. He thought a change of scenery would definitely distract her from thinking of the convent. However, Catherine's father wasn't giving her enough credit for her iron will, which he would realize later on. Catherine agreed to the proposal. She knew something had to change. Her obedience to God's plan through her father (even at her age) would reap positive benefits.

Paris was an absolute contrast to the familiar countryside and smallness of Fain. Catherine couldn't get used to it at first. Sure, the capital of France had its charm and beauty, but Catherine's new job was dealing with the very rough, uncultured workmen that frequented her brother's small restaurant. She had to turn her ear from the cussing, vulgarities, and rude remarks so commonly heard in the smoke-filled tavern atmosphere, though she had half a mind to confront them and teach them some manners. Catherine, in time, did succeed in meriting some respect from the illiterate patrons.

Catherine retreated to her heart constantly in prayer, never forgetting her beckoning vocation. Time seemed to waste away, however. The clock was ticking, and Catherine did not have a solid plan for entering the convent. She was miserable but offered everything to God and tried to be patient.

All too familiar with their father's rough demeanor, Catherine's siblings sympathized with her and began to scheme some kind of escape for her. Without Pierre's knowledge, the family was planning to move Catherine to the home of her brother Hubert and his wife, Jeanne, in Châtillon. Somehow they did work it out and got their father's blessing too—an intimidating task, to say the least.

At the same time, Catherine felt inspired to write to her sister Marie Louise, who was now the superior of the Sisters of Charity only six years after her novitiate. Catherine confided her desire to become a religious to Marie Louise. With encouragement and concern, Marie Louise answered Catherine's letter:

> If God begins to speak to your heart, no one has the right to prevent
> you from entering the service of so good a Master, which is the grace
> I beg Him to bestow on you…Therefore if God calls you, follow
> Him.[3]

Catherine's heart and soul felt refreshed upon reading her sister's affectionate letter.

The family was well aware that the three youngest children, Catherine, Tonine, and Auguste, did not have a formal education, nor were they taught very much about reading and writing at home. Their mother was a teacher but seemed to primarily teach them home-keeping skills and did not send them off to school. And so, the family concurred with Marie Louise's suggestion to spend time with their sister-in-law, to learn to speak French better "than they do in our village," and to improve her reading, writing, and arithmetic skills. Mary Louise also heartily encouraged Catherine to grow in "piety, fervor, and love of the poor."[4]

Catherine had to receive at least a basic education before entering the religious life. It was decided that Jeanne, Hubert's wife, would seek permission from Catherine's father for this arrangement. The cultured and educated Jeanne told her father-in-law, Pierre, that Catherine would benefit greatly by visiting with her and Hubert for an extended time. After all, Jeanne ran a boarding school for young girls from prominent families, and Catherine would certainly learn from the fruitful environment. Pierre gave his consent. Catherine would move to Châtillon.

FROM BAD BOYS TO LACE AND CULTURE

The unrelenting exposure to the offensive behavior of the men at her brother's eatery had been taking a toll, so Catherine was relieved to walk away from it, but she did feel like a fish out of water trying to blend in to her new surroundings in Châtillon. At twenty-three years old, her knowledge of reading and writing was pitiful and embarrassing. It wasn't her fault. She had previously gotten by without any proper schooling. Our Lord didn't require any schooling during her visits to him in the little Labouré chapel, the pigeons she fed back home couldn't care less whether or not she was learned, nor did it matter that she was uneducated when taking care of the spacious Labouré farmhouse. But the page was turning, and a new chapter in Catherine's life was about to unfold.

Jeanne Labouré, Catherine's sister-in-law, took every opportunity to take Catherine aside and give her private lessons so she might feel less embarrassed in front of the young girls attending the boarding school. Still, the primped and arrogant girls laughed at Catherine because she was so different. She was a country girl. She wasn't stupid. She might have been much brighter than many of the girls there—she merely lacked the education. Catherine disliked putting up with insults, but it ultimately strengthened her resolve to keep moving toward her dream of serving God in the convent, and it bolstered her spiritual life as well.

It turned out that Jeanne also had a love for the poor and the sick. She took Catherine with her to the Hospice de la Charité, run by the Sisters of St. Vincent de Paul, and introduced her to folks there. Catherine found respite in serving the sick with friendly visits.

One day Catherine visited the hospice to meet with the sisters' superior. As she sat in the parlor waiting for the sister to come down, Catherine spotted a portrait of an elderly priest on the wall. This wouldn't have been too surprising, because this sort of image can be seen in many convents, but what drew her in were the man's countenance and his penetrating eyes. Where had she seen this priest? It was the priest from her dream! At this point she could hardly sit still, but she mustered up every bit of calm she could and waited for the superior.

When she arrived, Catherine asked, "Sister, who is that priest?"

"Why, my child, that is our holy founder, St. Vincent de Paul," the sister responded in a matter-of-fact tone.

Catherine forced herself to contain her amazement and simply went on with a conversation with the sister. At her first opportunity, however, Catherine met with her confessor, M. Vincent Prost, and spilled the beans about her baffling dream and seeing the unsettling portrait four years later. Without skipping a beat, M. Vincent Prost immediately said: "I believe, my child, that this old man is St. Vincent de Paul who calls you to be a Daughter of Charity."[5] Catherine knew then that St. Vincent de Paul was to be her father.

Trying to Get There

If St. Vincent de Paul was calling Catherine, she realized, certainly he would make sure it happened in the way our good Lord had intended. She need not worry about the details, even though she was concerned about what her father would say about it. Although she was old enough to make decisions for herself, she was raised to be respectful of her parents, and she had only one living parent to please right now—the less accommodating one.

Catherine tried to avoid leaving for the convent without her father's blessing. God only knows how things might have been different if her mother, Madeleine, were still in the picture. In spite of everything, Catherine reminded herself that her adopted Mother Mary would indeed pull all of the necessary strings.

Mary must have been working overtime because more than one obstacle had to be dealt with before Catherine could be free to comply with St. Vincent de Paul's beckoning. First, her sister-in-law Jeanne approached Pierre about Catherine's innermost desires to become a nun. Pierre gave his consent—reluctantly. He made it clear, however—perhaps because he was angry or worn down—that he wouldn't be providing a dowry for his daughter. It must have been extremely sad for Catherine to hear—after all of the devotion she had shown toward her father, he had cast her off in this way. Yet, Catherine never outwardly complained about it, nor did she ever speak ill of her father.

Nevertheless, the lack of a dowry from Pierre wouldn't put a stop to Catherine's vocation, because Jeanne and Hubert promised to supply it.

Thankful for this promised gift, Catherine wanted to seize the moment, so she headed over to the hospice to see the superior. She still had to convince the sister to accept her as a postulant in her order.

Catherine's lack of education was a problem. In the short time staying with Jeanne and Hubert, Catherine didn't learn enough to convince anyone that she had higher than a first- or second-grade education. Sister Josephine Cany was new in her position as superior there and was not so sure she should take on such a difficult candidate.

In God's providence, Sister Francoise Victoire Sejole came to the rescue. She was the assistant of the house. Though humble and unassuming, Sister Sejole was supernaturally gifted with discerning the hearts of others. In addition to her seeing Catherine's pure heart and intentions, she also had spent time with her when making the rounds to serve the sick.

Sister Sejole implored Sister Cany to receive Catherine as a postulant. Sister Sejole promised that she would help Catherine learn her prayers and anything else she needed to learn. She added, "She is a good village girl, the kind St. Vincent loved."[6]

[C H A P T E R   T W O]

Where It All Started

CATHERINE COULDN'T BE HAPPIER. SHE would finally enter the convent of the Daughters of Charity (also referred to as the Sisters of Charity), who were known for their love for the poor and their cheerful presence all around Paris. In fact, Catherine had a special connection with St. Vincent de Paul already, since she made her first Holy Communion on the day that is celebrated by the Vincentian Fathers, otherwise known as the Congregation of the Mission founded by St. Vincent de Paul, as the birth of their community.

In 1633 St. Vincent de Paul, along with St. Louise de Marillac, had founded the first order of sisters that would mingle with the townspeople and not be restricted to the secluded contemplative life of the convent. It began when a young, country peasant woman named Marguerite Naseau happened to cross paths with St. Vincent de Paul. St. Vincent was so impressed with her way caring for and teaching poor girls that he became inspired to start the Daughters of Charity. Around this time, in 1625, St. Louise de Marillac was seeking spiritual direction from St. Vincent. So, Vincent asked Louise to meet Marguerite and to get involved with her Confraternity of Charity. About four years later, both being inspired to do so, Vincent and Louise had collaborated to found a new community of women, the Daughters of Charity.

We learn from the Constitutions that "[the] principal end for which God has called and assembled the Daughters of Charity is to honour Our Lord Jesus Christ as source and model for all charity, serving him corporally and spiritually in the person of the poor."[7] St. Vincent de Paul had preached of the need for this love for the poor:

You must also remember that your principal concern which God asks especially of you, is to be very attentive in seeing the poor, who are our Lord's.... You must see that, as far as in you lies, they want for nothing, both with regard to their physical health and the salvation of their souls."[8]

St. Louise de Marillac similarly expressed:

It is not enough to visit the poor and to provide for their needs; one's heart must be totally purged of all self interest.... We must continually have before our eyes our model, the exemplary life of Jesus Christ. We are called to imitate this life, not only as Christians, but...to serve Him in the person of His poor.[9]

Shortly before St. Louise's death, she reminded the sisters to take great care in their service of the poor and to live together in a true community life. As a final wish she added, "Pray hard to the Blessed Virgin, that she may be your only Mother."[10]

More than a hundred and fifty years after St. Louise uttered those zealous words of encouragement to take Mary as one's Mother, Catherine modeled well this call throughout her life. In fact, Catherine unknowingly followed Louise in this closeness to the Blessed Mother. St. Louise was born out of wedlock on a feast of the Blessed Mother (August 15, 1591) and never knew her mother. She was later shunned by her father's new wife, Antoinette. Louise claimed Mother Mary as her own mother, just as Catherine would do years later.

Although the Daughters of Charity eventually became a common sight on the streets of Paris, they weren't always so beloved. The original sisters to hit the streets were mocked and disliked by the Parisians, even though their entire vocation was centered on serving. Despite a slow start, the order grew to the thousands. In time, people came to accept the sisters and recognized their worth, calling them, "Mothers of the Poor," "Angels on the Battlefield," and "Swallows of Allah."

Today we might think that the sisters may have looked a little out of place donning their oversized, starched, white headdresses and long, voluminous, blue habits, hoofing the streets of Paris in search of the needy, while hauling their signature huge market baskets overflowing with foods and medicines. One might even wonder if a sudden wind gust would cause the sisters to blow away! Yet, in reality, St. Vincent de Paul wanted the sisters to dress as the peasant women in France at that time, and the women wore these types of headdresses.

Later on, when Pope Pius XII (who reigned from 1939 to 1958) recommended advancements in the outdated dress of some religious communities of women, he made exceptions for the cornette or white headdress of the Daughters of Charity. Even though someone who had never before encountered the sisters might do a double take, the pontiff explained that "it has become the universal symbol of charity."[11] And so it remained an essential part of their religious habit. But more recently the sisters have found the cornette to be too cumbersome (especially when getting in and out of cars), so it was put aside in the 1960s.

It's important to note that in 1809, St. Elizabeth Ann Seton embraced the apostolic life of St. Louise de Marillac and St. Vincent de Paul and founded the first congregation of religious sisters in the United States and called it the Sisters of Charity of St. Joseph. With just a few variations, she modeled it after the Daughters of Charity and devoted the order to the education of the poor and to teaching at parochial schools. From these roots grew a huge Catholic parochial school system in the United States. St. Elizabeth had originally wanted to join the Daughters of Charity of St. Vincent de Paul, but the embargo of France due to the Napoleonic Wars prevented her from doing so, and she began her own order instead. However, in 1850 the community took the necessary steps to merge with the Daughters of Charity, becoming the first American branch.

Today, almost twenty thousand Daughters of Charity serve the poor in ninety countries. Their ministry is not limited to the ways of the 1600s or even the 1800s. They are committed to meeting the needs of the people in each time, particularly the poor and marginalized (prisoners, abused, homeless, elderly, and more), through their social and humanitarian work. Over the years, as society's needs evolve, the Daughters of Charity have continually adapted their ministries to meet the needs all around them. "In all their ministries, the Daughters of Charity find the face of Christ in the people they serve. They spend their lives loving their neighbors!"[12]

BIDDING GOOD-BYE AND SAYING HELLO

Catherine was more than ready—it was time to enter the new walk of life for which she had been yearning. With her father's halfhearted blessing, the superior's permission, and a dowry and trousseau of clothing from Hubert and Jeanne, on January 22, 1830, Catherine Labouré said good-bye to her family and friends and walked through the doors at the Hospice de la Charité in Châtillon-sur-Seine.

Catherine's postulancy was somewhat as she had anticipated. She rose early at 4:00 AM with the sisters and participated in every part of their day—the meals, prayers, recreation, study, and many chores. In addition, she accompanied the sisters on their rounds to the homes of the poor. Catherine especially held dear the sisters' practice of going into the chapel each day at 3:00 PM to prayerfully honor the time of Jesus's passion, begging Jesus by the merits of his death to help the poor, sinners, and the souls in purgatory.

This new postulant put her heart into everything she set out to do, both at the convent and while out and about serving the poor. Catherine's loving actions were noticeable to others who observed her cleaning, cooking, praying, and serving others with great care and attention. She didn't draw attention to herself, but there was indeed a certain glow about her countenance and a pure love that exuded from her—simple, humble, and holy.

Sister Sejole kept her promise and taught Catherine reading and writing and everything else she needed to learn, each day. Catherine excelled in her education in this setting, which was such a contrast to her hardly learning a thing at her sister-in-law's elegant boarding house. She was at peace here and ready to learn. Throughout the short lessons and upon observation, Sister Sejole could see a beautiful depth to Catherine's spirituality as well.

Three months of postulancy flew by, and Catherine was ready to enter religious life. She would now be known as Sister Labouré and would start her novitiate period, which was also called "the seminary." Catherine was warmly welcomed into the convent by the mistress of novices at the motherhouse on Rue du Bac in Paris. Although Catherine kept a calm exterior, she was thrilled as she walked about the convent, receiving the unpretentious tour and instructions from the mistress of novices.

The country lanes, rolling fields, farms, and pastures of Fain were now a vivid and pleasant memory, and Catherine could finally put down roots in her piece of heaven on earth where she would lovingly serve her Lord. No matter what difficulties might lie ahead, she thought, she would possess peace of heart. Her dream had become a reality at last.

Not long before Catherine settled into the convent, the people of France had suffered through the horrible French Revolution and the Reign of Terror of 1793. The two religious families founded by St. Vincent de Paul were forced to go underground for a time to avoid persecution. But just because the Vincentian priests and Sisters of Mercy couldn't be found at the seminaries or convents didn't mean they weren't serving the poor. They still bravely ministered to the needy though times were fierce, doing so incognito in common street clothes.

However, because Napoleon was well aware that the sisters had such a prominent nursing ministry in France, he finally allowed them to locate at a motherhouse on the Rue du Vieux-Colombier. The clever sisters pressured Napoleon to allow their brothers, the Vincentians, to take up a residence, too. It took some time, but four years later the priests were allowed to return to Rue de Sevres. Then in 1815, the sisters moved to Rue de Bac, where Catherine entered the convent.

So, when Catherine arrived at the motherhouse, some thirty years after the Revolution, the sisters were still feeling the pinch. Their habits didn't match one another: most were black, and some were blue. A few years later, Mother General Boulet proposed an offer to an unemployed weaver she met. He was given a monetary advance, and the sisters would again be able to wear the traditional royal blue habits, thanks to the weaver's expertise.

Though things were in a bit of disarray after the sisters had reclaimed their proper place in France, there was excitement in the air. Sister Labouré couldn't have arrived at a better time. She would be present to experience something remarkable that was about to unfold.

Unearthed Relics

Interestingly, right at this time the relics of St. Vincent de Paul were scheduled to come out of hiding and be solemnly enthroned to the high altar of his church in the Rue de Sevres, which was close to the sisters. There was still a bit of unrest and fear in France because of the anti-religious sentiments that still prevailed. When the French army was planning to attack Algiers, the archbishop of Paris, Monseigneur de Quelen publicly invoked the intercession of St. Vincent de Paul, (knowing that the saint had once been a slave in Algeria) asking him to bless the arms of France. The Holy See then approbated him to authorize the solemn translation of St. Vincent's relics to occur on April 25, 1830.

St. Vincent de Paul's relics had been hidden away during the Revolution to keep them safe from the horrendous acts that were committed by the French, including desecrations. St. Vincent's body was preserved from harm since it was moved from place to place throughout the Montagne–Ste. Genevieve quarter. Then finally, on the feast of the Assumption, August 15, 1815, he was brought home to rest at Rue de Bac by the sisters.

King Charles X and the royal family attended the ceremony at the Cathedral of Notre Dame. Pontifical vespers were sung at two o'clock in the afternoon, and following that a novena was recited in honor of St. Vincent, whose body was clothed in majestic vestments and enshrined in a solid silver case. Afterward, the massive assembly of religious orders—including the Sisters of Charity—clergy, civic officials, and the faithful, accompanied by the archbishop of Paris, left the cathedral and processed down the streets to the saint's own church. The streets were lined by the common people coming out to watch. And walking very humbly along with the other sisters in procession was Sister Labouré, an unknown saint—one saint celebrating another. But, really, who knows? There may very well have been other saints not yet known or canonized present as well.

For nine days, each afternoon the Vincentian priests at Rue de Sevres would celebrate a pontifical Mass and a solemn novena service to St. Vincent de Paul. Day after day thousands of Parisians packed the church to venerate the relics and to invoke St. Vincent's intercession through the novena. The king returned home on the fifth day of the novena.

Sister Labouré partook in the festivities and prayers along with the sisters each day. She found them to be very far removed from the simple Masses back in Fain. She took every bit of it in, delighted to celebrate the order's founder, begging from him that God's holy will be manifested in her life and asking him to teach her what she should pray for. Sister Labouré began to open up to St. Vincent during her prayers, asking him to care for both the orders he founded and for France as well.

St. Vincent's Heart

Sister Labouré was now becoming more aware of the founder of her order. He was the one she had fled from in her dream years ago and whom she later observed in a frame on the convent's wall. Now, he seemed bona fide to her after she participated in the pontifical Masses and ceremonies and in particular after her prayers of novena to him. He was about to become even more real.

The sisters kept a shrine of St. Vincent in their chapel, which contained a bone from his right arm, the one he would use to bless. God only knows how many blessings came from that arm. Even in death it was blessing still. One night after getting back from novena prayers said at the Vincentians', Sister Labouré knelt in the chapel to pray. Suddenly, St. Vincent's heart, white and hovering above the shrine, appeared to Sister Labouré. She understood this colored heart to mean peace and unity for the two communities that St. Vincent had founded.

The next evening, St. Vincent's heart came again to Sister Labouré in another apparition. This time the heart was fiery red. She immediately grasped the symbolism in her own heart, taking it to mean that the community would be renewed with fervor and devotion, extending to the ends of the earth.

On the third evening, Sister Labouré was blessed once again with a vision of St. Vincent's blessed, passionate heart. This time, though, she was immediately saddened because the heart was a dark red color, and she knew that somehow this meant deep suffering for herself and for the king of France. She understood that there would be a change of government and that she would have to endure great anguish in overcoming hindrances.

Then Sister Labouré heard a sad but somehow reassuring message spoken to her interiorly: "The heart of St. Vincent is profoundly afflicted at the great misfortunes which will overwhelm France."[13] Perhaps the message was reassuring even as it was distressing, because it was proof that her founder was intimately connected to and cared for his two families even from heaven.

St. Vincent's heart, in various colors, continued to appear to Sister Labouré about ten more times in the evenings after she returned from praying at the Vincentians' church. When the solemn novena came to a close, St. Vincent's heart appeared to be a vermillion color, and Sister Labouré recognized it as a sign of celestial happiness. Sister Labouré interiorly knew that St. Vincent's prayers had been heard and that the Blessed Mother had prevented evils that would have befallen France. Sister Labouré's confessor, Father Aladel would later speak of this in a conference he delivered two days before he died in 1865.

The heart of St. Vincent had been hidden away during the strife of the French Revolution and was then enshrined in the Cathedral of Lyon. In 1947 the Mother General of the Sisters of Charity begged Cardinal Gerlier, archbishop of Lyon, to allow the sisters to bring their founder's heart to their shrine during festivities at the time of St. Catherine Labouré's canonization. Cardinal Gerlier granted the request, and the founder's heart was brought to rest in an impressive reliquary placed in almost the exact spot where the apparitions had appeared to Sister Labouré. Mother Blanchot's request merited more than a temporary grant, for the holy heart remains there today.

Sister Labouré was blessed with many graces during the nine-day solemn novena to her founder, but she also felt intense responsibilities heaped upon her shoulders. Sister Labouré was very new to the novitiate, and as much as she would rather not discuss what had happened during the apparitions for fear of being ridiculed or not believed, she knew she had to. She made an appointment to see her new confessor as soon as possible.

What would Father think or say? He was a young priest, only about seven years Sister Labouré's senior, and was known to be on the ruthless side. Sister Labouré just spilled it out quickly to Father Jean Marie Aladel. She had no other choice.

He told her to forget about it.

Sister Labouré prayed hard, went about her duties in the convent, and accomplished everything she was supposed to do wholeheartedly. But how could she just forget about what had happened?

Another Great Grace

While Sister Labouré was "forgetting" about the apparitions of St. Vincent's heart, she was granted another great grace. She saw the visible presence of Jesus in the Blessed Sacrament all throughout her novitiate. She tried not to believe she was seeing the visions—not doubting the true presence of Jesus in

WHERE IT ALL STARTED

the Blessed Sacrament, but not wanting to admit to herself that she was be
granted another grace. It was the prudent thing to do, she thought. This way
she could prevent possible illusions.

The visions of Jesus in the Blessed Sacrament persisted. There was no way
she could ignore them. On Trinity Sunday, June 6, 1830, during the Gospel
at Mass, Christ the King came to visit Sister Labouré. He was gloriously robed
as a king. No sooner had he presented himself to her, unexpectedly all of his
royal ornaments fell to the ground, his cross dropping under his feet. Sister
Labouré's heart descended into a deep sadness. She realized the message at
once. There was to be a change in government, and King Charles X of France
would be stripped of his royal trappings.

It is remarkable that the King of Heaven would come to earth to foretell the
falling of an earthly king. But then again, the ancestry of royalty in France was
rooted in Rome and went back to A.D. 800, when Charlemagne was crowned
by the pope on Christmas day. We can ponder the possible messages of the
vision, but Sister Labouré knew what it meant to her and was very aware that
changes in France's government in the past had caused much suffering.

Sister Labouré again told her confessor what she had seen. Once again, he
dismissed her vision, and she suffered interiorly because of this. Sister Labouré
was being tested and purified as saints often are. She went about her business,
trusting in God and being obedient to her duties. God was preparing her for
what would be coming next.

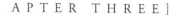

O NE NIGHT, THE EVE OF the feast of St. Vincent de Paul, July 18, 1830, Sister Labouré headed off to bed with her heart brimming with joy. Just a bit earlier that evening in the chapel, after giving a lesson on devotion to the saints and particularly their founder, Mother Martha gifted each of the novices with a small piece of a vestment that St. Vincent had worn. Sister Labouré held hers tightly in her hand and prepared for bed. She knew something was about to happen very soon.

Lying in bed in her quiet room, she prayed to St. Vincent, pouring out her heart to him once again. She had grown so fond of this special saint who seemed to have adopted her as his own. Sister Labouré looked forward to morning Mass, when she would deeply celebrate on his feast day the sheer gift of St. Vincent in her life. Then, Sister Labouré felt suddenly inspired to rip her petite cloth relic in half and swallow half of it as an act of devotion. She instantly felt an overflowing, deep peace. Somehow she knew—*Tonight I shall see her*, she mused. Sister Labouré was soon asleep.

T HE F IRST M IRACULOUS V ISIT: "T HE V IRGIN OF THE C HAIR"
The flickering light of a candle lit up Sister Labouré's room a couple of hours later.

"Sister Labouré!"

She was still groggy. The small child carrying the candle gently approached her bed. An intense heavenly radiance caused the child's white gown and hair to glow luminously, which together with the candle's glow made the room as bright as the noonday sun.

"Sister Labouré!"

She started to stir. The brightness and the child's voice calling to her drew her out of a sound sleep.

"Sister Labouré!" The third time, she opened her eyes—wide—and looked intently upon the child holding the lit candle, light beams bouncing off of him.

"Come to the chapel. The Blessed Virgin awaits you."

Sister Labouré was completely at peace. She knew this little child would be taking her to see her Mother—the Mother of God—the one she claimed as her Mother many years ago. She had no reason to fear or wonder why she would receive such a blessing, but she was concerned that others in the convent would see them. After all, there was a great light around the child. It couldn't be missed!

"Do not be uneasy," the child reassured her. "It is half past eleven; everyone is asleep. Come, I am waiting for you."

Sister Labouré dressed more quickly than she ever had before in her life. Even in her haste, she put her habit on as impeccably as it should be, fastening every last button, smoothing out its fabric. In no time at all, she was spruced up and ready to accompany the heavenly child to go see her Mother.

Sister Labouré followed the child's cues and headed after him out her doorway, fascinated that the lights in the hallway were all lit and shining brightly. She neither saw nor heard anyone as she followed the little child down the hallways and stairways toward the chapel.

The heavy chapel door, which was locked, opened wide with ease when the child simply touched it. Sister Labouré was again amazed to see splendid light. The chapel was lit up as brilliantly as if Midnight Mass were about to start! The altar had been dressed in crisp linens and adorned with flowers in preparation for the great feast day tomorrow.

The young novice was directed by the small child to come forward toward the sanctuary. He then paused by the superior's chair. Sister Labouré knelt down spontaneously. All was calm. She could smell the candles burning and hear little creaking sounds in the quiet, old chapel. But nothing happened. No one was there. Sister Labouré questioned herself and glanced toward the child. It must be real. It couldn't be a dream.

"Here is the Blessed Virgin."

Instantly, Sister Labouré heard the swishing of a silken gown. She immediately focused in the direction of the sound and observed a lady descending the altar steps. The lady sat down on the superior's chair. Could this really be her, she wondered. She looked a little like St. Anne. The little child read her thoughts.

"This is the Blessed Virgin."

The lady looked at her. The reality of the Blessed Mother's presence hit Sister Labouré, and she immediately threw herself at Mary's knee and rested her hands gently on Our Lady's lap. Sister Labouré caught her breath and raised her eyes to peer into her Mother's delightful face. This would be the sweetest moment of Catherine's whole life.

"My child," the Blessed Mother began. "The good God wishes to charge you with a mission."

Mary had more to tell Catherine. "You will be tormented," she explained, "until you have told him who is charged with directing you. You will be contradicted, but do not fear, you will have grace. Tell with confidence all that passes within you; tell it with simplicity. Have confidence. Do not be afraid."

Sister Labouré gave the Blessed Mother her full attention, savoring the miraculous experience of being with Mother Mary. She took in every single word and would be able to repeat them later on.

"You will see certain things: give an account of what you see and hear. You will be inspired in your prayers; give an account of what I tell you and of what you will understand in your prayers."

The Blessed Virgin revealed prophecies about world events. "The times are very evil. Sorrows will come upon France; the throne will be overturned. The whole world will be upset by miseries of every kind." Her holy face appeared distressed.

Mary lovingly shared the secret to heavenly help. "Come to the foot of the altar," showing Catherine the spot. "There, graces will be shed upon all, great and little, who ask for them. Graces will be especially shed upon those who ask for them."

The focus turned to the two communities, the Vincentians and the Daughters of Charity. Mary expressed to Catherine that she loved her community. "My child, I particularly love to shed graces upon your community; I love it very much."

Yet Mary was saddened by these communities, too. She told Sister Catherine that rules were not being observed by both of the communities. "Tell that to him who has charge of you, even [if] he is not the superior. He will be given charge of the community in a special way; he must do everything he can to restore the rule in vigor. Tell him for me to guard against useless reading, loss of time, and visits."

With all that said, the Blessed Mother also made an encouraging promise: "The community will enjoy a great peace; it will become large."

The Virgin Mary enlightened Sister Labouré about the extraordinarily awful miseries that lay ahead but emphasized the grace and protection Sister Labouré would receive. "There will be an abundance of sorrows; and the dangers will be great. Yet do not be afraid; tell them not to be afraid. The protection of God shall be ever present in a special way—and St. Vincent will protect you. I shall be with you myself. Always, I have my eye upon you. I will grant you many graces."

Then Mary repeated her words, emphasizing her message. She added, "The moment will come when danger will be enormous; it will seem that all is lost; at that moment, I will be with you; have confidence. You will recognize my coming; you will see the protection of God upon the community, the protection of St. Vincent upon both his communities. Have confidence. Do not be discouraged. I shall be with you."

Mother Mary revealed more specific heartaches. She paused often as she told them to Sister Labouré, softly weeping in between broken sentences. "It will not be the same for other communities. There will be victims... There will be victims among the clergy in Paris. Monseigneur the Archbishop..." Mary paused, her face distraught. "My child, the cross will be treated with contempt; they will hurl it to the ground. Blood will flow; they will open up again the side of Our Lord. The streets will stream with blood."

Mary hesitated and stopped speaking. Then, after sighing, she concluded, "My child, the whole world will be in sadness."

Sister Labouré could only wonder when this might happen, and before she could think of asking, she understood with great clarity that it would occur in forty years.

After that, Mary seemed to fade away. Sister Labouré rose from her knees. The holy child led her out of the chapel and toward her room. Catherine's heart was changed forever—filled with joy, confidence, peace, and a great sorrow intermingled. She had just been with the Mother of God! She felt as if she could have floated back to her room. But, no, her feet were firmly on the floor as she followed her guide back to her room. How she would get back to sleep was a question she couldn't answer.

She reached the side of her bed, and the child then faded from her sight as the Blessed Virgin had. Suddenly, Sister Labouré understood that the child was her guardian angel, and it made her smile to think that her guardian angel who because of her prayers knew all about her secret desire to one day see the Blessed Mother had helped it to come about. The clock struck two, and Catherine realized that she had been with the Blessed Mother for two whole hours. In a way, it seemed like time had frozen still when she knelt before her Mother, her hands resting on her lap. Though Mary and her guardian angel had faded away, Sister Labouré had no doubt whatsoever that she had indeed experienced a miraculous occurrence. It was real—very real. She couldn't sleep the rest of the night.

Only a week later, a revolution erupted, on July 27, 1830. It was an intense and bloody but short-lived battle. People were left dead in the streets. Monseignor de Quelen went into hiding, aided by the Sisters of Charity. As the Blessed Mother predicted, the Vincentians and the Sisters of Charity were spared from harm. Angry mobs assailed the community house of the priests twice and both times left without a skirmish. King Charles X retreated to England, and Louis Philippe took the throne. Life was different, but life went on.

Sister Labouré had been to see Father Aladel to tell him all about the Blessed Mother's visit before the battle had taken place. How could Sister Labouré have known about such things without heavenly assistance? Father had a lot to think about. As horrendous as the revolution had been, it did in a sense vindicate what Sister Labouré was talking about. Father Aladel had to believe her now. Would he?

Sister Labouré had also told Father Aladel that the Blessed Mother wished for him to establish the Confraternity of Children of Mary. The Blessed Mother had promised many graces and indulgences. The month of May should be celebrated with great solemnity. "Mary loves festivals," she said. "She will reward their observance with abundant graces." But Father Aladel didn't act upon this request until five years later, in 1835. And it would be seventeen years after the Blessed Mother made the request that the Children of Mary would become an official pontifical association by Pius IX.

The Second Visit: "The Virgin of the Globe"

She couldn't forget it. The Blessed Mother had told Sister Labouré that she was to be entrusted with a mission. Was it to warn Father about the revolution? Would Sister Labouré be blessed with seeing Mary again? She wondered about that, and she prayed constantly as she fulfilled her daily duties in the convent, doing everything as she should.

On the day before Advent was to begin, the Sisters of Charity were headed to the chapel for their evening meditation. Evening meditation was a prayerful time welcomed by Sister Labouré. The long day of duties was coming to an end, and there was a respite of time to catch one's breath and meditate and pray. With Advent beginning the following day, November 28, 1830, there was a lot to think and pray about and for which to prepare her heart.

Then she heard a familiar sound. There could be no mistake. Sister Labouré plainly heard the swishing of silk like she had heard four months earlier. She could see Mary, the Mother of God, standing on a globe in the sanctuary! Sister's heart was pounding with happiness. Mary was back "in all her perfect beauty,"[14] as Sister Labouré would recount later on.

Catherine's eyes were glued to her holy Mother. She would later recount every last intricate detail of Mary's attire—the "white veil" on Mary's head that fell on "either side to her feet," and "under the veil her hair, in coils, was bound with a fillet ornamented with lace, about three centimeters in height or of two fingers' breadth, without pleats, and resting lightly on the hair." The brilliant light all around the apparition that evening was beyond dazzling. The Blessed Mother was holding a golden ball. She raised her eyes heavenward and seemed to offer it to God.

Suddenly, Catherine could see the many magnificent rings adorning Mary's fingers—"three rings on each of her fingers," all of them shimmering with precious gems while cascading beams of light. Then, Mary looked straight into Catherine's eyes and said, "The ball which you see represents the whole world, especially France, and each person in particular."

Sister Labouré pondered the loving words. Mary went on: "These rays symbolize the graces I shed upon those who ask for them. The gems from which rays do not fall are the graces for which souls forget to ask."

OUR LADY OF THE MIRACULOUS MEDAL

Mary stretched her arms out wide. She had a look of compassion in her eyes, and rays of light poured out of her fingers upon the globe under her feet. The golden ball she had previously held was gone now. Instantly, an oval frame appeared, surrounding the Blessed Mother. Sister Labouré saw words that were written in gold around the edge of the oval: "O Mary, conceived without sin, pray for us who have recourse to thee."

Our Lady said to Catherine, "Have a medal struck after this model. All who wear it will receive great graces; they should wear it around the neck. Graces will abound for persons who wear it with confidence."

Sister Labouré took each word in and instantly memorized Mary's instructions. The image spun around slowly, and she could see the other side of the sizeable oval. A large letter *M* was surmounted by a bar and a cross, and right beneath it was the heart of Jesus crowned in thorns and Mary's heart pierced with a sword. Twelve stars encircled the entire image.

The vision then faded at once. Sister Labouré would later describe it: "Everything disappeared from my sight, like a candle that is blown out."

Sister Labouré remained in a mystical ecstasy. The next thing she remembered was being in the dining hall with the others. She heard the mistress of novice's voice matter-of-factly say, almost as if she were annoyed: "Sister Labouré must still be in ecstasy." Of course, the mistress of novices didn't really suspect that Catherine was in any sort of ecstasy but was merely being sarcastic. Yet, she was absolutely correct!

Sister Labouré may have been a bit embarrassed, and she didn't even remember how she got to the dining hall. But she quietly picked up her fork and ate her meal as she pondered the miraculous apparition. She felt calm and peaceful, but at the same time she felt as if she could burst, knowing that her holy Mother had entrusted her with so great a mission.

As soon as time allowed, Sister Labouré met with Father Aladel to tell him all about what had happened in the chapel. She begged Father to keep what she was about to tell him a complete secret from everyone else. She felt a bit reluctant to pour out her heart to him since he never took her seriously, always dismissing her visions, but she knew she absolutely needed to disclose everything because the Blessed Mother was counting on her.

Just as she thought, Father Aladel didn't take her seriously. At least, he didn't appear to. Sister Labouré, out of obedience, respected her confessor but knew she had to somehow convince him. She put the whole matter of the apparitions of the medal aside as Father instructed, only having another vision occur to her, and another! All in all, Mary appeared about five times with instructions to have the medal made.

Each time, Sister Labouré was compelled to step forward and approach Father once again. She did so with trepidation and trembling, as the sisters who outlived her later testified. Sister Labouré would bring up the subject in the confessional, which was very wise of her, keeping it all within the holy confines of the sacrament. The sisters outside the confessional could sometimes overhear Father Aladel's firm commanding tone of voice toward Sister Labouré and heard sister trying her best to plead her case.

There was even a time, which Sister Labouré testified to many years later, shortly before her death, when Father Aladel called her a rude name. Sister had confessed to him that she told the Blessed Mother that she "had better appear to someone else, since no one will believe me." She said that Father was horrified and called her a "wicked wasp!"

Father Aladel would later testify that Sister Labouré was never disobedient or rebellious. He said she was quite submissive. Sister Labouré had always been strong willed. She was a strong farm girl at heart, after all. But she learned early on to use her will for good purposes to glorify God. The Blessed Mother must have been well aware of Sister Labouré's iron will and was surely confident that despite the obstacles, Sister would get her point across to Father Aladel.

Discerning God's Will Takes Time

What should Father Aladel think? Was she out of her mind? Anything worthwhile takes time. Discerning God's will sometimes takes a very long time. The Church has to be absolutely sure about the authenticity of an alleged heavenly message or apparition before confirming it. Beginning with Father Aladel, who had no easy task trying to discern what to do with Sister Labouré, and on through the whole Church process, God was at work—even though, in Sister Labouré's mind, receiving acknowledgment from Father Aladel seemed to take forever.

There was much for Father to digest and unravel, and he had to do it alone because Sister Labouré had insisted that he tell no one. She was exceedingly mindful of Mary's instructions to tell this "to him who has charge of you." The timing was challenging for him, too. Everything happened shortly after Catherine entered the novitiate, when the relics of St. Vincent de Paul were being solemnly enshrined. Adding to the mix were the civil and religious unrest and the eventual change of government. It was difficult enough to keep up with all of that.

The fact that Sister Labouré was a simple country girl with very little education was compelling, since this made her unqualified intellectually to make up something like this. The fact that her predictions came true also weighed on Father's mind.

Eventually, the story got out. There were murmurings around the convent that the Blessed Mother was appearing to some sister there. Apparently, it was Father who had leaked some of the details about the apparitions, even though he didn't believe them. But Sister Labouré never let on that it was she who received the privileged visits from the Queen of Heaven. It was challenging, but she kept her lips sealed. Rumors persisted for years about Sister Catherine being the chosen one. Many times, Sister Catherine or Father Aladel was approached and asked straight out if it was Sister Catherine. Sister always had a good comeback, a giggle, a startled look, or a piece of advice.

Later, there was a priest, Father Villette, who slipped a little when appointing Sister Dufes to be the superior of Enghien by alluding to the fact that the seer lived there. And Sister Sejole, who had helped get Catherine accepted into the convent, would at times make remarks about Sister Labouré's holiness. But Sister Catherine ended up keeping her secret for forty-six years!

Being Sent Forth

The novitiate period of study was coming to an end, and the sisters would be assigned to a post. Father Aladel had to somehow make sure that Sister Labouré would not be transferred far away, because he knew he still had work to do discerning the apparitions, but the matter of the post was really beyond his jurisdiction. Yet, by God's grace and the Blessed Mother's intercession, Sister Labouré was assigned to the Hospice d'Enghien located at Reuilly in Paris, and Father Aladel was the confessor there, which worked out perfectly.

During a visit to the rue du Bac, after being settled in at her new post at Enghien, the Blessed Mother came to Catherine for the last time in an apparition. Mary looked the same as when she had become visible on November 27, but instead of being to the left of the sanctuary, as before, she appeared directly above the high altar. The Blessed Mother told Sister Labouré, "You will see me no more, but you will hear my voice in your prayers." For the next forty-six years, Sister Labouré and the Mother of God would continue their conversation naturally and secretly.

In their conversations, the Blessed Mother complained to Sister Labouré that nothing was being done about the medal.

"But, my good Mother, you see that he [Father Aladel] will not believe me."

"Never mind," the Blessed Mother responded. "He is my servant, and would fear to displease me."

Sister Labouré had to tell him this. Father Aladel was deeply troubled by her message, which echoed in his soul. The Blessed Mother was speaking of her displeasure—and that Father would be fearful to displease her. And he was. He trembled at the thought of it—at everything that had been laid upon his shoulders. The fear that the Blessed Mother spoke of was precisely what compelled Father Aladel to act. Father would never want to displease or disappoint Mary. This recent sentiment expressed by Mary certainly shed new light upon the entire situation.

[C H A P T E R F O U R]

Medal of the Immaculate Conception

NOW, WITH ALL OF THE responsibility heaped upon his shoulders, Father Aladel confided in his friend Father Etienne without revealing that Sister Labouré was the one who had received the holy messages. Together they concluded that Sister Labouré was trustworthy and absolutely solid in her faith.

In January 1832, Father Etienne took Father Aladel with him while making an official visit to Archbishop de Quelen, who happened to have a strong devotion to the Immaculate Conception of Mary. After Father Etienne finished the scheduled business, Father Aladel had the opportunity to tell the archbishop about his penitent, her visions, and all of Mary's messages to her. The archbishop took it all in and then questioned Father Aladel about Sister's character. He also wanted to hear every detail about the proposed medal to discern whether or not it was theologically correct.

Archbishop de Quelen was very satisfied with what he heard and pleased that the medal adhered to what the Church taught and was rich in symbolism regarding Church doctrine. He gave his stamp of approval for the medal to be made, requesting that some of the first medals be sent to him.

An outbreak of cholera besieged the area, and, alas, the striking of the medal was further delayed; ironically, acts of mercy were the cause. The Sisters of Charity were front and center in their efforts to care for the sick. Father Aladel was entirely inundated in directing the sisters during the life-threatening epidemic.

God's ways are mysterious. But we can look back and perhaps see that the timing of the holy Medal, although thought to be late in coming, providentially became a reality in the month of Mary—May 1832. Father Aladel met with the engraver and ordered twenty thousand medals.

The intended design for the Medal was to be from the first part of the great apparition of November 27, called the "Virgin of the Globe." The approved design ended up being an image of the second part of the great apparition of November 27, representing Mary bestowing graces through the rays that fall from her outstretched hands onto the globe that is under her feet. Later on, Sister Labouré would comment on this change of design when she wrote an account in 1876. But she seemed completely happy with it at the time that the Medals were made and voiced no complaints.

Many years later, Sister Labouré's last director, Father Chevalier, would explain the reason he believed was behind the change of design. In a deposition to the Beatification Tribunal, when Catherine's case to be beatified was being examined, Father Chevalier made clear that the first design was too difficult to represent in metal. In 1832, all kinds of metals couldn't be etched in such detail. Father Chevalier understood that Father Aladel deferred to the engraver's advice regarding which phase of the apparition to create.

The two phases had different emphases on doctrine. The first phase of the apparition honored Mary in her Immaculate Conception and expressed that Mary is the mediatrix of all graces, which means that Mary presents all of our prayers to God (whether we pray to God, the angels, or the saints). As well, all graces that are answers to prayers or that are gifts from God pass to us through Mary's hands. That's why the Church calls her the "mediatrix" of grace. And so, the first phase of the apparition, which showed Mary praying, looking toward heaven, and offering the golden ball of the world to God, expresses Mary's intercession for all of us. The rays flowing from her fingers show God bestowing graces through the Blessed Mother.

In the second phase of the apparition, we see only the bestowal of the graces through the rays of Mary's extended hands. We understand the graces to be from God but coming to us through Mary. The whole element of Mary offering our prayers to God in intercession for us, which is illustrated in the first phase as she offers the golden ball of the world to God, is not shown in the second phase. Yet, we can comprehend that the rays of grace coming from Mary are because she has interceded for us.

The medals were made. The front side presents Mary in the glory of her Immaculate Conception standing on a globe, as the Queen of Heaven and Earth. Her feet are crushing the serpent, showing that Satan and all of his followers are helpless before Mary's power. Mary is an intercessor—the rays of light come from her hands to symbolize the gifts and graces coming through her intercession to all who ask for them. Around the rim is the invocation that Mary composed, "O Mary, conceived without sin, pray for us who have recourse to thee."

The reverse side of the medal presents Mary in her relationship to the Church. There are no words. Two hearts, an *M,* and a cross intertwined with the *M* are shown, with twelve stars around the edges. Mary told Sister Labouré that words were not needed: "The *M* and the two hearts express enough." The back of the medal expresses that Mary is queen and intercessor, Mother of the Redeemer, but also our Mother who knows our sorrows. Mary is with us throughout the sorrows of our lives, and so the heart of Jesus wears a crown of thorns and Mary's heart is pierced with a sword. The *M* intertwined with the cross expresses Mary at the foot of the cross of her Son. The twelve stars remind us of the twelve apostles, representing the entire Church as it surrounds Mary. We are also reminded of the stars in St. John's vision, when "a great sign appeared in heaven, a woman clothed with the sun, and the moon under her feet, and on her head a crown of twelve stars" (Revelation 12:1).

Finally, on June 20, 1832, the first two thousand medals from the order of twenty thousand were delivered. Not one to sit back, the foremost thought uttered from Sister Labouré upon receiving her first medals was: "Now it must be propagated."

Miraculous Propagation

The first supply of twenty thousand medals, which were called "medals of the Immaculate Conception," was distributed so quickly that it almost seemed miraculous in itself. Pope Gregory XVI placed a medal on his desk at the foot of his crucifix. Archbishop de Quelen received his batch of medals, put one in his pocket, and set off immediately to visit the former chaplain to Napoleon, Monseigneur de Pradt, the archbishop of Malines, who was on his deathbed. He had previously refused visits from Archbishop de Quelen.

Monseigneur de Pradt had been excommunicated by the Holy See because he had sided with Napoleon and remained unreconciled with the Church. Hoping to aid Monseigneur before he departed from this earthly life, Archbishop de Quelen attempted to speak with him. But Monseigneur refused to discuss his excommunication and the sins that caused it.

They bid their good-byes, and the archbishop headed out, saddened that Monseigneur would most likely die without the Church's blessing. Suddenly, Monseigneur de Pradt called back the archbishop. The graces of Our Lady of the Miraculous Medal were acting. Monseigneur became wholly repentant and made a complete confession, and he was received back into the arms of his Mother, the Church. The following day, the ill Monseigneur died a peaceful death. His miraculous, sudden change of heart was considered the first signal grace of the Miraculous Medal.

CHAPTER FIVE

Miracles and Marvels of Grace and Health

WHEN THE MEDAL OF THE Immaculate Conception first came off the presses, it seemed it couldn't be passed out quickly enough. People were anxious to have one, having heard they were from the Queen of Heaven. As well, extraordinary and miraculous wonders were happening that were attributed to the medal. As the medals were handed from one person to another, people began to say, "Here is a Miraculous Medal." In a short time the "Medal of the Immaculate Conception" became known as the "Miraculous Medal," and the new name stuck.

The first twenty thousand medals had spread all over France and beyond. People were wearing the medal and clinging to the hope of the Blessed Virgin's promises to listen to their prayers. Amazing things happened. Hardened sinners began to repent, hearts were transformed, the seriously ill were cured, peace dwelled in places it had not before, and there were countless conversions to the faith. Folks were looking for Miraculous Medals, not as lucky charms or a form of superstition, but as marvelous sacramentals of the Church that would bring them graces to cope with the ills of life. There was no other sacramental of the Church that had yet had such an influence on the faithful since the rosary, which was responsible for thoroughly defeating the Albigensians and Turks.

The Blessed Mother must have been very pleased with the design of the medal, since so many favors were bestowed on those who wore it. It would be impossible to record all of the favors and miracles that occurred because of the Miraculous Medal. But in 1833, Archbishop de Quelen was aware of countless miracles occurring, so he decided to have some recorded. He commissioned a well-known theologian, Father Le Guillou, with the task of scrupulously examining all reports of the remarkable favors that were attributed to the Miraculous Medal. In April 1834, the miracles were verified and noted in a publication called "Mois de Marie," for which Father Aladel wrote the introductory letter. The brochure's first edition sold out on the first day. Future editions sold out quickly as well.

In the same year, Father Aladel wrote a ninety-page book called *The Miraculous Medal,* which went into four editions within the year. The once-skeptical priest was now spreading the story of the Miraculous Medal. Further new editions, which had grown to almost three hundred pages, were released in 1835, 1836, and 1837. In 1842, an eighth edition was over six hundred pages long. The ninth edition wasn't printed until 1878, after Sister Labouré's death, and contained a biography of her.

Archbishop de Quelen appointed Monseigneur Quentin, vicar of Paris, to conduct a canonical inquiry and opened sessions in 1836. Sister Labouré was found to be of high character and virtue. The Miraculous Medal was found to be of supernatural origin, and the miracles worked through it authentic. This meant that the Miraculous Medal was given solemn ecclesiastical approbation. Since the ecclesiastical court was held only a few years after the apparitions, firsthand witnesses were available to testify, which was extremely vital to the Holy See's approbation of the medal as well as to the establishment in 1895 of a feast in honor of the Miraculous Medal. Further, this work was extremely beneficial for Sister Labouré's beatification in 1933.

Hundreds of millions of Miraculous Medals were made and distributed within the first forty years after the Blessed Mother had given the gift of the medal. Mary's graces were at work. Archbishop de Quelen developed a series of pastoral letters urging the faithful to become devoted to Our Lady of the Immaculate Conception. He consecrated himself and his diocese to the Immaculate Conception. He consecrated the church of Notre Dame de Lorette in Paris on December 15, 1836, to "Mary honored in her most pure conception." Through Mary's intercession and Archbishop de Quelen's efforts, the invocation "Queen conceived without sin" was inserted into the Litany of Loreto.

Nearby to the Sisters of Charity on Rue du Bac lived a parish priest named Father Desgenette, who belonged to the parish of the Church of the Missions. Father Desgenette was very inspired by the recent happenings and suggested that Father Aladel welcome pilgrimages to the Chapel of the Apparitions on Rue du Bac. Father Aladel flatly refused, stating that the sisters needed quiet in order to live out their spiritual life properly. And since the Blessed Mother had not specifically asked for pilgrims to come, Father Aladel felt there was no need. He suggested that Father Desgenette welcome pilgrimages to his own parish.

Father Desgenette didn't take him up on the idea. It didn't seem sensible, since the Blessed Mother hadn't appeared there at his parish. In 1832, he was appointed pastor of the rundown and neglected parish of Notre-Dame-des-Victories. He had his work cut out for him. For years he toiled trying to get a spark ignited in the parish. It was very discouraging because the parish was empty most times. People were disinterested in the sacraments, sometimes even at the hour of death. Father Desgenette was about ready to give up trying. But Mary's graces were working again, and on December 3, 1836, he sensed an interior illumination during Mass that flooded his heart and soul with peace. He was told to dedicate his parish to the Immaculate Heart of Mary.

As soon as Mass was finished, though, a twinge of uncertainty entered Father Desgenette's heart—he suddenly wasn't sure if what he had heard was real. But no sooner than he doubted, he heard the same voice again telling him to dedicate his church to the most holy Immaculate Heart of Mary. Father went over to the rectory and decided to ponder what set of rules he would compose for an association in honor of the Immaculate Heart of Mary. As he wrote, his pen seemed to do the writing. The thoughts so unambiguous in his mind came out perfectly on his paper. He knew without doubt that he was being divinely inspired.

In less than a week, on December 11, Father Desgenette announced that he was forming a new society and would hold the first meeting that evening. He hoped and prayed that he would get about fifty folks interested enough to come out. Five hundred, mostly men, showed up! During the meeting, they recited the Litany of Loreto. At the invocation "Refuge of Sinners, pray for us," which Father recited three times, those gathered experienced a surge of devotion.

It was miraculous. Archbishop de Quelen canonically erected the Association of the Holy and Immaculate Heart of Mary for the Conversion of Sinners just five days later. A total transformation swept through the parish like wildfire. The once-neglected parish became a place of national pilgrimage. A couple of years later, on April 24, 1838, the association was raised to an archconfraternity and had the power to affiliate similar associations.

The archconfraternity of Notre-Dame-des-Victories became the lifework of Father Desgenette, who had listened to and acted upon the interior locution to consecrate his parish. At the time of his death, the members in the archconfraternity numbered twenty million with fifteen thousand affiliated confraternities. The numbers have grown enormously since that time.

It might be interesting to ponder that, about a century later when some were considering Father Aladel's refusal to allow pilgrimages to the convent of the Sisters of Charity on Rue du Bac, it was feared that perhaps his refusal prevented the spread of the Miraculous Medal devotion in an even greater way, as the Blessed Mother might have intended. In addition, the sisters were deprived of the opportunity to welcome any faithful pilgrims who would have wanted to flock there. However, Father Desgenette picked up the slack, and because he did, the faithful were deeply inspired by visiting the shrine he established. Whether Father Aladel's decision was for the best or not, the Queen of Heaven saw to it that the chapel at Rue du Bac would indeed eventually become a place of pilgrimage and would be called the "Chapel of the Apparitions."

From France to Rome

Something fascinating happened in 1841 to bring attention to the Miraculous Medal in the secular world, which also resulted in Rome's officially recognizing the medal. This event centered on a twenty-eight-year-old man named Alphonse Tobie Ratisbonne, a wealthy Jewish lawyer and banker who possessed a hatred toward Catholicism, especially since his older brother left Judaism to become a Catholic priest.

Alphonse became engaged to a young Jewish aristocrat and decided to take a trip to Malta before tying the knot. He left Strasbourg on November 17 and arrived in Naples in December. He spent time socializing with his Jewish friends. For some unknown reason, the ship that Alphonse planned to sail home on kept holding off its departure. So, he decided upon another route through Palermo; but by mistake, he showed up to the Rome window of the ticket office. He had never wanted to step foot in Rome because of his hatred for Christianity. Irritated because of the constant delays and now this mistake, however, he booked his trip to Rome and sent word to his friends to expect him back in Naples on January 20.

As Providence would have it, Alphonse arrived in Rome on January 6, checked into his hotel, and bumped into an old friend. His friend, Gustave Bussieres, introduced Alphonse to his brother, Baron Bussieres, who happened to be a recent convert to Catholicism.

While in Rome, Alphonse was a typical tourist and checked out the sights, which ended up disgusting him since he loathed the Church. He quickly booked a trip out of Rome. Before leaving, he paid a short visit to his friend's home. When arriving at Baron Bussieres's home, the doorman instinctively showed him in. When the Baron learned that Alphonse was about to leave Rome, being an enthusiastic new convert, he let loose a last-ditch effort to try to save Alphonse's soul. That was the last straw, and Alphonse refused to put up with it. He was filled with rage and hostility and began to bash Catholics, blaming them for the mistreatment of the Jews.

Baron pulled out a Miraculous Medal and simply challenged Alphonse to wear the medal and pray the *Memorare*. It couldn't hurt, right? Strangely enough, Alphonse went along with the challenge and even permitted Baron's young daughters to place the blessed medal around his neck. Because Alphonse didn't know the prayer, Baron gave him his and asked that Alphonse copy it and return the original to Baron (even though Baron knew the prayer by heart). Alphonse copied it by hand, and as he did the words stayed with him. He couldn't get them out of his head. He later said it was like an opera song that gets stuck in your head and you begin singing it over and over in your mind.[17]

While out one evening, the Baron saw his old friend, the Comte de la Ferronnays, at a dinner at the Palazzo Borghese. He decided to tell him about recently giving the medal to Alphonse Ratisbonne, and his friend promised to pray for his conversion. The Comte went to the basilica of Santa Maria Maggiore with his wife to pray his *Memorares*. After praying more than twenty and entrusting the situation to the Blessed Mother, he went home. Shortly after arriving at his home, he had a heart attack and died.

Then one night, Alphonse saw a vision of a cross without a corpus, which disturbed him to the core of his being. The next day, Alphonse set out to finish bidding farewell to his friends and happened to cross paths with Baron Bussieres as he was on his way to the church of Sant'Andrea delle Fratte to make funeral arrangements for the Comte de la Ferronnays. He told Alphonse that Ferronnays had prayed for him, which compelled Alphonse to accompany Baron to the church. Instead of just waiting in the carriage as Baron suggested, Alphonse went into the church to look around at the architecture while Baron took care of business in the sacristy.

Suddenly, a large, aggressive-looking black dog appeared in the church, right in front of Alphonse, blocking the way in front of him. Then, unexpectedly, the dog disappeared. Immediately, a surge of resplendent light emanated from the chapel of the guardian angels which was to the left of the nave. When Alphonse looked up, his eyes met the compassionate eyes of the Blessed Mother, who was in the exact same pose as on her Miraculous Medal. Her arms were outstretched, her hands pointed down, and brilliant rays of grace streamed from them. He could only look at the blinding beauty of her eyes for a minute at most. He then focused on her hands. No words passed Mary's lips. None were necessary. Alphonse said he "understood all."[15]

Alphonse fell to his knees, and Baron found him there when he came out of the sacristy. As Baron helped him up, Alphonse quietly said, "Oh, how that gentleman prayed for me!"

After all of the excitement, Alphonse practically floated back to his hotel, where he immediately sent for a priest and begged to be baptized. Later that night, he felt compelled to keep vigil by the Comte de la Ferronnays's body at the church. Then, after attending the funeral, Alphonse began a ten-day retreat run by the Jesuits. He remained in Rome and studied the Catholic faith with Father de Villeforte.

One man's journey into the Church is never exclusively his own, for everyone's life—for better or worse—has to have some sort of ripple effect on others. Alphonse's conversion was of international significance since he was known far and wide within diplomatic and financial circles for his hatred of the Church. Alphonse received the three sacraments of initiation into the Church—the sacraments of baptism, confirmation, and Holy Eucharist—from Cardinal Patrizi at the Church of the Gesu. The grand ceremony was well attended.

News of Alphonse Tobie Ratisbonne's miraculous conversion from Judaism to Catholicism reverberated all around Rome and then throughout Europe. Until this time, the Miraculous Medal was only approbated by the archbishop of Paris. But when word got out about Ratisbonne's remarkable change of heart and the alleged involvement of the Miraculous Medal, Rome instituted an official inquiry into his conversion. Cardinal Patrizi officiated the twenty-five sessions that took place between February 17 and June 3, 1842. The Church rendered her decision. The court "fully recognized the signal miracle wrought by God through the intercession of the Blessed Virgin Mary, in the spontaneous and complete conversion of Marie Alphonse Ratisbonne from Judaism to Catholicism."[16]

Alphonse made several attempts to speak with the visionary who had been given the task of propagating the Miraculous Medal but was told that the sister insisted upon being unknown. Even Pope Gregory XVI wasn't able to speak with Sister Labouré when he expressed an interest, for that matter.

The man who hated the Church with a passion went on to spend ten years with the Jesuits, studying for the priesthood. He asked to go to China to evangelize but was turned down repeatedly. Believing he was meant to be an apostle, Alphonse joined his brother, Theodore, who had founded the Congregation of Our Lady of Sion in order to evangelize the Jews. Alphonse spent over thirty years in the Holy Land, passionately evangelizing his own people.

Meanwhile, more prayers were answered and graces bestowed upon the two communities. Father Etienne was elected superior general in 1843 and for years took up the task to reform the order as the Blessed Mother had requested.

Adjusting to Convent Life

While all of the logistics of making the Miraculous Medal were being worked out and the wonders that ensued were coming to fruition, Sister Labouré was deeply entrenched in convent life and all it entailed. She was involved in cooking, cleaning, and taking care of the sick. If you think Sister Labouré might have been swimming in consolations since she was the chosen one, think again—nor was she given special privileges in the convent. She never divulged that she was the one who had received the messages from the Blessed Mother. She was trained and treated as any other sister would be. In fact, she experienced her share of troubles and then some.

Convent life meant being relentlessly subject to a superior, who at times may be unreasonable in her demands and expectations. Sister Labouré had many superiors to answer to during her postulancy, novitiate, and beyond. Like all of the other sisters, Sister Labouré had to bend her own will to God's will by being obedient to her superiors. This in itself was a great trial for Catherine, who had always possessed an iron will.

In addition, her new life would entail living in community with others whom she probably wouldn't have chosen to live with. The sisters might end up working side by side in the kitchen or infirmary with others who have quirky habits, act unkindly, or simply rub one the wrong way—sometimes even to a breaking point. Yet, mysteriously, within the give and take and contradictions of everyday life in the convent as well as through heroic efforts and doses of God's grace, saints are made.

Just as Sister Labouré had slipped out of the Labouré farmhouse in Fain to visit with Jesus in the Blessed Sacrament at the church across the lane in between her chores, she found immense spiritual respite whenever she could steal away to the chapel at the convent to kneel before our Lord. She was known to strip off her white apron, enter the chapel, bow toward the tabernacle (in those days women didn't genuflect), and then look toward the statue of the Blessed Virgin, pausing for a moment or two to drink in graces from our Lord. Sister Labouré prepared for each Holy Communion (which she received three times per week) with the utmost love and attention, striving to perform all of her actions the day before with perfect love for Jesus.

Whenever the occasion presented itself, and if Sister Labouré was free to do so, she would visit with her brothers who were in Paris. They would see her at the convent, or she would go to them if they were sick and couldn't travel to see her. Sister Labouré couldn't take the long trip home to Fain to see her father, her brother Auguste, or her sister Tonine.

At a very simple vow service, on May 1, 1835, Sister Labouré pronounced her holy vows of poverty, chastity, obedience, and a fourth vow of stability, a promise to care for the poor in the community of St. Vincent de Paul for the rest of her life. Though the service was unembellished, it was a momentous occasion for Sister Labouré—the one she had waited for all her life. Her religious name would be Catherine, the name of her baptism. Every twenty-fifth of March, the feast of the Annunciation of Mary, the vows would be renewed. The Sisters of Charity are, in fact, laywomen living in community, not religious nuns, so the nature of the vow ceremony was private. St. Vincent designed the order in this way so that the sisters would be present to the poor in the world and not confined to the cloister.

After her father, Pierre, and brother, Auguste, died in 1838, Tonine married, settled in Vizerny, and had two children, Marie and Philippe. In 1858, Tonine and the family moved to Paris, and she and her sister Catherine had the blessing of being close by to one another again. When Philippe was only fourteen years old, he learned to read Latin, and Aunt Catherine seized the opportunity to ask him if he had considered a vocation as a priest. Philippe told her that it had entered his mind but he couldn't be sure. That simple answer was good enough for his Aunt Catherine, who arranged for Philippe to attend the College of Montdidier conducted by the Vincentians, and arranging for her friend to pay for the education. He ended up spending several years at the college, with his invested aunt hovering over him, reminding him of the financial investment and not to let it go to waste.

At one point, Sister Catherine showed her nephew a piece of a cassock from a Vincentian priest, Jean-Gabriel Perboyre, who was martyred in China in 1840. She asked if he would consider entering the community of St. Vincent. She continued to plant the seeds in his heart. One day, Aunt Catherine began to very nonchalantly prophesize Philippe's future. She told him that if he wished to enter the community, the priests would be happy to receive him; he might even become a superior and go to China as well. She wouldn't pressure him; she merely planted the seeds with a smile.

Philippe did enter the Vincentians, and everything his aunt had casually foretold came to pass.

Sister Catherine also took other family members under her wing. For instance, one of her brothers strayed away from the Church, and Sister Catherine asked her niece Leonie Labouré to let her aunt know if he fell ill. She wanted to be sure he wouldn't die without the last sacrament of the Church. Also, Tonine's husband was at odds with the Church, so Sister Catherine kept after him, telling him she was praying for him and encouraging him to pray, too.

Sister Catherine was shocked and deeply saddened when her older sister Marie Louise, who had been superior at Castelsarrasin and a role model to her for so many years, suddenly left her religious community. It was no small thing, and Catherine took it upon her own shoulders to do all in her power to talk sense into her sister. She prayed through tears constantly and wrote several letters to Marie Louise, even sending her a letter that she had written to Catherine before Catherine entered the convent. It all seemed to no avail. Marie Louise would not budge in her decision to leave the convent and go back to the world. A stubborn will was a trait that ran through the Labouré family. But with God's grace a strong will can be used for tremendous good, and Catherine persisted.

Sister Catherine continued to trust in God and never stopped praying for her sister. When more than ten years had passed while Marie Louise was living away from the community, Sister Catherine felt compelled to send out another letter to Marie Louise. Soon after the letter went out, Sister Catherine felt overwhelming joy rush into her heart. Her prayers were answered: her sister returned to the community.

MARY, HER MOTHER

Sister Catherine carried on continual conversations with the Blessed Mother. She often answered Father Aladel's questions, and sometimes she would ask Mother Mary for advice on what she should do about particular situations.

There was a garden statue of Mary before which Sister Catherine would pray when she could, usually after she had fed the pigeons. One morning at four o'clock, when the bell rang for the sisters to rise, one of the sisters noticed that Sister Catherine was not in her bed and hadn't slept in it all night. The superior was informed, and a search for her ensued. They found her kneeling in front of the garden statue, her arms outstretched as if accepting something. Sister Catherine had been in the garden all night and was unresponsive. But suddenly she came out of her ecstasy, quite embarrassed that she was being watched, and got right up on her feet.

In 1850, Pius IX pronounced that the Blessed Mother was "preserved and exempt from all stain of original sin, from the first instant of her conception." Certainly, the apparitions of the Miraculous Medal to Catherine Labouré in 1830 paved the way for the solemn declaration of the Immaculate Conception in 1854. Shortly after, in 1858, Mary appeared to the young peasant of the French Pyrenees, Bernadette Soubirous. Mary told her, "I am the Immaculate Conception." Sister Catherine was overjoyed when the news reached her, saying, "You see, it is our own Blessed Mother, the Immaculate!"

Not only are both apparitions linked to the Immaculate Conception, but both are linked to the Miraculous Medal as well. Bernadette Soubirous (now St. Bernadette, canonized on December 8, 1933) wore a Marian medal when Mary appeared to her. Her medal was a kind of replica of the Miraculous Medal. The front was identical to the Miraculous Medal, but the back of it was devoted to St. Teresa of Avila. Her medal is preserved in the archives of Rue du Bac.

GRACE UPON GRACE

The Blessed Mother had further business to attend to at the convent at Rue du Bac. In 1840, toward the end of January, the Queen of Heaven visited the house again. It was during retreat exercises. Sister Justine Bisqueyburu, who had entered the novitiate on November 27, 1839, the ninth anniversary of the apparition of the Miraculous Medal, was praying in a prayer hall behind the Chapel of the Apparitions on January 28, 1840. As she prayed, she saw the Blessed Mother suddenly appear, wearing a long, white dress with a blue mantle. Her head was bare, as were her feet. She held her Immaculate Heart, pierced with a sword, in her hand. Throughout the course of the retreat the vision was repeated several times to Sister Justine, and later, as well, on all of the Blessed Mother's feast days.

On the feast of Mary's nativity, September 8, 1840, the vision appeared again but this time with additional elements. Mary was carrying her Immaculate Heart in her right hand, and hanging from her left hand was a scapular of green cloth. An image of Mary as she had appeared in the other apparitions to Sister Justine was on the front of the cloth. On the reverse side was an image of a heart, pierced with a sword, surmounted by a cross, and afire with brilliant rays. Surrounding this were the words, "Immaculate Heart of Mary, pray for us now and at the hour of our death."

Father Aladel had his hands full. Now another sister had approached him with a mind-boggling story. Sister Justine was compelled to disclose the details of her visions to Father as Sister Catherine had done. She, too, met with the same difficulties in not being taken seriously regarding having a scapular, or "cloth medal" made (since it is worn like a medal and consists of only one piece of material, not two as a scapular is comprised of). After several complaints from the Blessed Mother to Sister Justine because her gift to the community was not taken seriously once again, Sister Justine sought help from Monseigneur Affre, archbishop of Paris. After about six years, in 1846, the distribution of the "Green Scapular" occurred at last.

Even before the Green Scapular was distributed, in 1845 the Blessed Mother was again bestowing her unrestrained graces on the community. Sister Appolline Andreveux began receiving visions of Jesus in his Passion at her convent at the Hospice de Saint Jean Troyes throughout the year. Then, on July 26, 1856, Jesus appeared to Sister Appolline holding a red scapular. On one side was an image of Jesus on the cross, surrounded by all of the instruments of the Passion. There were the words: "Holy Passion of Our Lord Jesus Christ, save us." The other piece of cloth contained images of the hearts of Jesus and Mary, surmounted by a cross, with the words: "Sacred Hearts of Jesus and Mary, protect us."

Sister Appolline confided the details of her visions in writing to Father Etienne and the superior general. The approbation for making the scapular was granted during the same audience in 1847 when Pius IX approved the Confraternity of Children of Mary. There can be no doubt that heaven was looking favorably upon the community.

Record, Medal, and Promise Keeping

Being obedient to Father Aladel's instructions, in 1841, Sister Catherine wrote up a full account of the apparitions. Upon finishing her written account, she sent an unsigned note to Father. She was extremely cautious when she put anything in writing to Father about the apparitions because she didn't want anyone who might by chance come upon it to know it was she who was the visionary. The note to Father Aladel reiterated what she had asked him time and time again. She emphatically explained that she had for ten years felt compelled by the Blessed Mother to tell him that an altar to the Blessed Mother must be erected on the spot she had appeared. Mary had promised that everything asked for at her altar would be granted. Further, Sister Catherine asked Father to establish a special "Communion" day to be celebrated by the entire Community each year as well as a special day in memory of St. Vincent's heart. She emphasized that God would be glorified, the Blessed Mother would be honored, and that indulgences would be granted.

Sister Catherine also reminded Father Aladel that the Blessed Mother was still awaiting a commemorative statue of the first phase of the apparition, an image of her holding the golden globe in her hands and offering it to God. It was not erected until after Sister Catherine's death. And, many years later, the commemorative Communions she requested in 1841 were finally decreed by the superior general. Also, although Sister Catherine would not live to see Our Lady's altar become a reality, it was erected four years after her death, in 1880.

At one point, Sister Catherine was called in to see the superior of her community, who told her that she wanted her to consider being a superior. Sister Catherine was greatly opposed to the idea and gently protested. The superior never bothered her about it again.

On May 1, 1860, in an intimate celebration with the sisters, Sister Catherine, fifty-four years old, observed the twenty-fifth anniversary of her vows. She was the senior sister in the house. That was the year that Sister Jeanne Dufes, thirty-seven years old, was appointed the superior of the Revilly and Enghein house. Father Etienne mentioned to Sister Dufes that Sister Catherine Labouré was leading a hidden life at the house. Why he alluded to Sister Catherine being the seer, we can only guess. But it seems that Sister Dufes had something against Sister Catherine right from the start. Sister Dufes went out of her way to humiliate Sister Catherine in front of others and at times severely reprimanded her.

Besides the account she wrote in 1841 at the request of Father Aladel, Sister Catherine was commanded again in 1856 and 1876 to write full accounts of her visions. The Church often requires this of a visionary in order to preserve religious history and so that the accounts can be studied later on when considering beatifications and canonizations. Catherine was diligent in including many intricate details of the apparitions, which she described eloquently.

Throughout the rest of her life, Sister Labouré would keep some of the first medals with her. About ten of the original Miraculous Medals are preserved in archives in Paris with the Daughters of Charity. One of the original medals can be seen at the Miraculous Medal Art Museum in the Germantown neighborhood of Philadelphia.

Eternal Life Was Approaching

Sister Catherine was not one of those saints who longed for death. She had been a diligent worker, full of life. She selflessly cared for the elderly men at Enghien, getting on her knees to scrub floors (even as the arthritis in her knees plagued her), answering the door, never missing a beat. She didn't want death to come too soon and planned on waiting for God to determine when it would be. But her health was deteriorating, and in 1874 Sister Catherine was officially relieved of her duties as the custodian of the house of Enghien and of her service to the elderly men in her care. In 1876, Sister Catherine began alluding to her earthly life as ending soon. On each feast day, she said she wouldn't be there to see the next and certainly wouldn't be there in 1877.

Known for her common sense, levelheadedness, and understanding of deep spiritual matters, Sister Catherine would often give advice, such as, "Be calm; do not be disturbed," and, "Let us allow the good God to work. He knows better than we what is needed."[17] She followed her own advice as she approached the time of her death.

Then, around May 1876, Sister Catherine, knowing she would be leaving this earth soon, became increasingly more concerned because her spiritual director, Father Chinchon, had been transferred, and she was now left in a lurch regarding carrying out the remainder of her mission. Sister Catherine felt compelled to tell Sister Dufes that if the Blessed Mother gave permission, she would tell her about the apparitions.

The next morning she told Sister Dufes everything. They sat in the parlor for two hours. We can only imagine what must have been going through Sister Dufes's mind as she hung on each of Sister Catherine's words. She had been so harsh with Sister Catherine through the years, but Sister Catherine had never complained. Revealing her holy secret allowed Sister Catherine once again to request that the statue of the Blessed Mother in the first phase of the apparition be sculpted and placed in the chapel as the Virgin Mary had requested. After disclosing everything, Sister Catherine felt that she could die in peace, knowing Mary's request would finally be accomplished.

Sister Catherine's health began to deteriorate even more, and as the sisters began to talk of her impending death, Sister Catherine was asked if she was afraid of dying. Sister Catherine responded, "Afraid, Sister? Why should I be afraid? I am going to our Lord, the Blessed Virgin, and St. Vincent."

A couple weeks before Christmas, Sister Catherine retired to her room because of weakness. Then on December 31, 1876, Sister Catherine was very frail and showed signs that she would die soon. The sisters arranged for her to receive the sacrament of the sick. Sister Catherine was at peace and seemed incredibly joyful even in her weakness. She asked the sisters to recite the Litany of the Immaculate Conception near her. The sisters surrounded her bed all day long, and visitors came to see her as well. Sister Catherine had kind and loving words for everyone and even some personal instructions for some, and she passed out the remainder of her Miraculous Medals to those in the room.

At seven in the evening, Sister Catherine seemed to go into a deep sleep and then suddenly breathed her last with perfect peace. All those who surrounded her did not weep, but they were filled with indescribable emotions, confident that they had witnessed a saint pass from one world to the next. Photographs were taken of Sister Catherine. The sisters carried her body into the chapel so that the Blessed Mother could watch over her, and they surrounded her with roses and lilies.

When it was time for supper, the sisters went off to the refectory. Sister Dufes announced that there was no need to keep silence any longer since Sister Catherine had died. She no doubt wanted them to be privy straightaway to the fact that they had been breaking bread with a saint all this time. Sister Dufes proceeded to read them Sister Catherine's account of her visions. They sat on the edges of their chairs, too amazed to take a bite of their supper. Even with the rumors and guesses, no one had known for sure that it was Sister Catherine who had seen the apparitions of the Miraculous Medal.

The sisters kept watch over the next couple days and through the night, drawn to be near their beloved sister's side. They couldn't bear the thought of losing her to the grave soon and prayed that somehow they'd be able to keep her.

On the night before her funeral, as the clock chimed four o'clock in the morning, Sister Dufes heard a voice, "The vault is under the chapel of Reuilly."[18] Suddenly, she remembered that during the construction of the chapel a vault was made, a kind of storage room that had been boarded up and never used. At the time of construction, Mother Mazin did not have a specific purpose in mind but had the thought that it would come to good use someday. Since the funeral was to be the following day, in a fury the sisters prepared the vault and the necessary petition for permission to have Sister Catherine's body put to rest there.

At the time of Sister Catherine Labouré's death, very few people were aware that she was the sister that the Blessed Mother had appeared to and spoken to. Catherine had kept her secret for forty-six years. However, once she had died the news spread quickly, and the next morning crowds appeared—clergy, religious, laity—all lined up to pass by her coffin, wanting to be near a saint. Catherine Labouré had gone overnight from a humble sister hiding within her convent life to a public saint who ushered in the Marian devotion to France and beyond.

The sisters' prayers were answered, and permission was granted to use the vault for Sister Labouré's burial. On January 3, 1877, the feast of St. Genevieve, Sister Catherine was buried in the vault under the house in Reuilly.

The procession following the funeral Mass from the chapel at the convent to Reuilly was breathtaking. The assembly was comprised of students from the sister's industrial school, orphans, the Children of Mary carrying their banner, the young girls of the Society wearing their livery of the Immaculate Heart of Mary, parishioners, the sisters, and the clergy. The solemn Benedictus was chanted as the simple coffin, adorned in flowers representing purity, was carried toward its destination. The Magnificat was prayed along with other hopeful Marian prayers.

Upon approaching the entrance of the vault, the Children of Mary sang the holy invocation, "O Mary, conceived without sin, pray for us who have recourse to thee!" The poor that Sister Catherine had served so lovingly could now do something for their beloved sister. They placed a lovely crown on her tomb. The entrance of the vault was walled up to protect the grave, but there was a private opening on the other side connecting to the chapel.

The first miracle occurred just a few days after Sister Catherine died. So much like the healing of the paralytic at Capernaum, a family brought a ten-year-old boy, who had been unable to use his limbs since birth, to Catherine's tomb. He was lowered down into the vault by ropes. Just after the boy's body touched the stone, he stood up straight for the very first time in his life—completely cured!

Conversions, cures, and wonders continued to occur all over the world from the devotion to the Miraculous Medal. The sisters at hospitals offered the medals to patients to wear and sometimes placed them under the pillows of those resistant to the medal, telling the Blessed Mother that they were leaving the whole matter in her hands. Soon after receiving the medal, the ill and those on the verge of death had a change of attitude and asked to see a priest for confession, Holy Communion, or baptism. One sister remarked, "The Medal, so dear to us, is really miraculous, and the instrument by which we snatch from destruction souls that have cost Our Lord so much."[19] To this day, by Mary's intercession through the Miraculous Medal, emotional healings take place, the hopelessly ill are cured, and conversions continually occur.

In 1895 Rome was petitioned for a feast day in honor of Our Lady of the Miraculous Medal. The Prefect for the Sacred Congregation in the Vatican, Cardinal Masella, received the papers of petition and was very inspired and impressed. He called upon Father Fiat, the superior general of the Vincentians, and Mother Lamartine, superior of the Daughters of Charity, to begin the process of beatification for Sister Catherine Labouré.

Surprisingly, there was a bit of hesitation initially. But that was only due to the spirit of the rule, which caused the sisters and Vincentians to naturally recoil from glory. Catherine Labouré herself had remained hidden all her life. However, it didn't take too long to convince Father Fiat and Mother Lamartine to move forward, because Cardinal Masella told them that if they didn't act on it, he would do so himself.

The making of a saint truly takes a lifetime. After the saint's death, the official proclamation of sainthood may seem to take a lifetime, too. Yet, it was only fifty years after Catherine's death that official discussions began to ensue about the possibility of her sanctity. Still, the process did take a long time, being delayed for a period for some unknown reason. But then two important pieces to the puzzle suddenly fell into place, allowing the investigation to move forward. Cardinal Ehrle, former director of the Vatican Library, and Father Ojetti, ex-secretary of the Commission of Canon Law, who had both been excused from active participation in the sessions due to illness, came forward in a rather dramatic way. Even in their ill health—Cardinal Ehrle being unable to walk and Father Ojetti confined to his home with advanced paralysis—both asked to return to the Sacred Congregation of Rites to help with sessions, having heard that they were at a standstill. They were adamant and said, "The cause of Sister Catherine Labouré is the cause of the Immaculate Conception." Their statement amazed everyone, including the pope.

Over eighty years old and an invalid, Cardinal Ehrle was carried to the Vatican and read his spirited testimony of Sister Catherine. Father Ojetti said, "I can only use my right hand and my pen, and it is my will to make them serve to uphold the cause of the Immaculate Conception!"

There were priests and officials who worked extremely long hours to dot every *i* and cross every *t* as they prepared the results of a pile of paperwork and testimonies as to Sister Catherine's virtues. A unanimous affirmative vote was obtained for the cause of the Immaculate Conception. The following day the Holy Father then ordered the process to continue, and the decree on the virtues of Sister Catherine was prepared and approved by the pope.

RAISED TO THE ALTAR

Sister Catherine was beatified at St. Peter's in a beautiful ceremony on May 28, 1933. At the beatification, Pope Pius XI said, "To think of keeping a secret for forty-six years—and this by a woman and a sister!"[20]

After being buried for fifty-seven years, Sister Catherine's coffin was exhumed by order of the Church. Her coffin was transferred to Rue du Bac, where it was opened in the presence of doctors, civic officials, and the archbishop of Paris, Cardinal Verdier. All those present were amazed at what they saw when the coffin lid was lifted. Sister Catherine looked as if she was asleep. Her body had not discolored, her eyes were bluer than blue, and her limbs were supple. Catherine's body was declared incorrupt by the Church. She was transferred to the Chapel of Our Lady of the Miraculous Medal at 140 Rue du Bac and placed in a glass coffin at the side altar.

Fourteen years later, Sister Catherine was officially declared a saint, canonized by Pope Pius XII on July 27, 1947, only seventy years after her death. Pope Pius XII gave a poignant epitaph of St. Catherine:

> Favored though she was with visions and celestial delights, she did not advertize herself to seek worldly fame, but took herself merely for the handmaid of God and preferred to remain unknown and to be reputed as nothing. And thus, desiring only the glory of God and of His Mother, she went meekly about the ordinary, and even the unpleasant, tasks that were assigned to her in the bosom of her Religious family.
>
> She was always willing and ready to give diligent attention to the sick, ministering to their bodies and their souls; to wait upon the old and the infirm without sparing herself; to act as portress, receiving all with serene and modest countenance; to cook; to mend torn and tattered clothing; to carry out, in a word, all the duties laid upon her, even the unattractive and onerous ones. And while she worked away, never idle but always busy and cheerful, her heart

never lost sight of heavenly things; indeed she saw God uninterrupt-
edly in all things and all things in God.

Impelled by the urging of love, she hurried eagerly before the
tabernacle as often as she could, or before the sacred image of her
holy Mother, to pour out the desires of her heart and to make an
offering of the fragrance of her prayers. Accordingly, it was evident
that while she dwelt in earthly exile, in mind and heart she lived in
Heaven and sought, before everything else, to mount with rapid
steps to the highest perfection, and to spend all her powers in
reaching it. She loved the Sacred Heart of Jesus and the Immaculate
Heart of Mary with a special warmth of piety; and she was ever
on the watch to influence, by word and example, as many other
persons as she could to love Them.

And thus when she came to the end of her mortal life, she did
not face death with fear but with gladness. Confident in God and
the most holy Virgin, she took time to distribute, with a weak and
tremulous hand, the last of her Miraculous Medals to those standing
by, and then, content and smiling, she hastened away to heaven. [21]

The secret to St. Catherine Labouré's sanctity lay in her obedience to her walk
of life. Though she wanted with all her heart to please God and the Blessed
Mother, she didn't try to be something she wasn't. She didn't strive to be
successful in anything worldly. Her heart and soul were deeply immersed in
everything she did—whether it was in her humble farm chores in Fain, the
care of her family, ministering to the poor and sick, or custodial work in the
convent. She knew she should be faithful and obedient to her daily duties of
prayer and work, performing everything as perfectly as she could to please
God and ultimately to be a living example of holiness.

CHAPTER SIX

The Miraculous Medal, a Conduit to Mother Teresa's Friendship

JUST AFTER MASS ONE WARM summer day, my family ambled out of the chapel at the Missionaries of Charity Gift of Peace House in Washington, D.C. We slipped our shoes back on before moving into the foyer of the convent. As we stood there, I was attempting to grasp tight the blessings I had just received, being present in the same chapel with a living saint. I can't describe the feeling. I was also trying to allow a breathtaking image that I had just witnessed moments earlier to sink fully into my brain and heart. It was when Mother Teresa suddenly rushed over and gave my daughter Chaldea a huge hug, right after Chaldea had attentively genuflected in front of the Blessed Sacrament before leaving the modest chapel.

These were amazing blessings to be sure! I remember, as if it were yesterday, exactly where I was standing at the moment that Mother Teresa approached me, too. I was holding my young daughter Jessica securely in my arms when the door creaked open just across from where I was standing. The tiny, frail-looking nun, dressed in her white cotton sari trimmed in blue walked determinedly toward *me*!

After Mother Teresa spoke to me about my children she blessed us with gifts. First, Mother Teresa gave Jessica a blessed Miraculous Medal. Then she gave one to me, then Justin, and finally Chaldea. Mother Teresa kissed each medal before placing them in our hands. I remember kissing my medal and drawing it to my heart. We treasured our blessed medals—given to us by someone we considered to be a living saint.

What an amazing gift—to happen to visit the convent when Mother Teresa was visiting from Calcutta, India. Yet, the blessings of this surprise didn't end there. Further, the gifts that Mother Teresa presented to us were not merely one-time gifts—the blessed Miraculous Medals she gave us would bring us many blessings and graces in days, weeks, months, and years to come. In the following days, I felt interiorly prodded to send a letter to Mother Teresa to thank her for the Miraculous Medals and also for her time visiting with us at the convent. Looking back now, I realize the Miraculous Medals were the reason I ended up writing to Mother Teresa, so they, in fact, became the conduit to my ten-year friendship with this holy woman. Of course, only God knows that for sure, but it makes sense to me. After that first letter went out to Mother Teresa, she wrote back to me, much to my surprise, and over the next ten or so years, she sent me twenty-one additional letters. I was blessed to see Mother Teresa in person at least twelve more times in various parts of the United States.

About four years after I met Mother Teresa, I was expecting my fifth child and suffering from a heart condition and a uterine hemorrhage. Because of this, Mother Teresa sent me another blessed Miraculous Medal and encouraged me to wear it and to pray to the Blessed Mother. That was about twenty-two years ago, and I am still wearing that very same medal—which is getting quite worn looking but is still blessed and powerful nonetheless. I believe the medal brought me much grace as I struggled through that pregnancy. And, thanks be to God, my daughter Mary-Catherine was born safe and sound, much to the surprise of my doctor!

Some years into our friendship, I somehow made a decision to give out blessed Miraculous Medals as Mother Teresa had always done. The reason I say "somehow" is because I don't remember exactly why or how I started to hand them out, but very naturally the Miraculous Medals became meshed within my ministry of reaching out to mothers, women, and families at my book signings and speaking events, and as I sent out book orders to fill countless requests from all over the world. I kissed each medal and touched it to the special one I wear constantly that Mother Teresa gave to me. I then would either hand the medal to the person I had met or mail it to those who ordered a book. Also, whenever I became aware of various dire needs regarding debilitating or terminal sicknesses, I inquired whether or not I could send a blessed Miraculous Medal to the afflicted person.

One time when I went to St. Peter's Basilica in Rome, I was able to get a large amount of Miraculous Medals I had brought from home blessed by Pope Benedict XVI at his audience. I used them to pass out to those I met at my events and to send with book orders.

The following year, I traveled to Rome again and brought over a thousand blessed Miraculous Medals with me. On my last day there, I made a point to visit my beloved John Paul II's tomb at St. Peter's. It was a very busy day at St. Peter's with elbow-to-elbow tourists. Tears immediately streamed down my face when I finally made my way over to Papa John Paul's tomb and knelt down before it. It was during my second visit to Rome that I was able to visit his tomb. The tears came each time. I felt thoroughly convinced that by kneeling there at that holy place, I would receive many graces. They were just about palpable.

Since there were so many people milling around, the guards had to keep the lines of tourists moving. They asked us to move along. I did so, but I came back and knelt down again a short time later. I kept my head down and my eyes closed while I prayed, hoping I wouldn't be asked to move again. I wanted desperately to have a chance to place my Miraculous Medals on John Paul II's tomb if it were at all possible. Tears came again. I was soaking up the graces. I prayed earnestly to be given an opportunity to place the medals on the tomb: "Lord, if it is your will, please let it happen."

The crowd was thick, and the visiting hours for the tomb would be coming to a close. It didn't look likely that I would be able to get my earnest wish. But suddenly, a little break in the crowd appeared. I immediately prayed and then ventured over toward the guard. I asked him if he could possibly place my bag of religious items on the tomb. When I realized that he did not speak English, I motioned my question to him. Thankfully, he understood my request and signaled to me that I had to wait just a bit. So, I took my place on the floor, kneeling behind the barricade, and I continued to pray. In a short while, the young guard motioned for me to approach and hand him my bag. He set it down on the tomb. My heart was rejoicing. He left it there for a few seconds before picking it back up and handing it to me.

I thanked him profusely and began to exit the area, misty-eyed. But after taking no more than two steps, I turned around, faced the guard, and reached into my bag, drawing out a blessed Miraculous Medal. I kissed it and handed it to him. He kissed it and, with the same hand holding the medal, struck his chest twice as he said, "Seminarian, seminarian!" He was studying for the priesthood and was visibly excited to have been given the blessed Miraculous Medal. I could see tears in his eyes, too.

Joy exploded in my heart as I parted company with the young seminarian responsible for placing my medals on John Paul II's tomb. I have remembered him in my prayers. It was time to leave my beloved St. Peter's and head back to the Missionaries of Charity convent nearby, where I would hitch a ride to another Missionaries of Charity convent in Rome to meet with Mother Teresa's archivist about my writings on Mother Teresa.

The memory of standing at the second Missionaries of Charity door, waiting to be welcomed in, is vividly etched in my mind. I later enjoyed a very nice visit with the sister in charge of Mother Teresa's archives. I was privileged to spend time in their private chapel and further blessed to enter into Mother Teresa's bedroom, the room where she stayed whenever she visited her sisters in Rome. I knelt beside her bed. The rustic wooden structure and the simple blue-and-white-checked bedspread are engrained in my mind. Before I had entered the holy room, I had asked the sister if it would be all right if I placed my Miraculous Medals and religious items on Mother Teresa's bed.

I was granted the permission, and the bag of medals lay there as I prayed, resting my folded hands on her bed. Time stood still. Prayers ascended from my grateful heart.

My heart was so very full. I had been gifted with two beautiful opportunities to make the blessed Miraculous Medals even more special. I was thrilled that I would now be able to give out those Miraculous Medals, which were touched to very holy places, both the tomb of Pope John Paul II and the bed of Mother Teresa.

[CHAPTER SEVEN]

Modern-Day Transforming Miracles

THROUGHOUT THIS CHAPTER I WILL be sharing a variety of the encounters I have experienced with some of the people to whom I have given Miraculous Medals and true stories about the Miraculous Medal that have occurred to these people. These encounters and stories happen on ordinary days during run-of-the-mill circumstances, but with the Blessed Mother's grace these moments are transformed into extraordinary occurrences. Sometimes the transformations occur within someone's heart, their soul, or even their body. Only God, the Blessed Mother, the angels, and the saints know for sure how these miracles come about.

The practice of offering blessed Miraculous Medals to others has become very natural to me. My friend Judy and I were having lunch one day in downtown Cincinnati when a panhandler came up to our table and asked us for money. I gave him a blessed Miraculous Medal. A year or so later Judy told me, "I find it very inspiring that the first thing you thought to do was to give him a medal."

When I give them out, I have no intention to write about the experience or even to share it. But in writing this book to help inspire a devotion to the Miraculous Medal, I can't help but desire to tell you about them. Although the duration of the exchange of a Miraculous Medal might be only a few minutes, I believe that the benefits of the encounter will last forever. I certainly do not profess that any one of these stories is a report of an authentic, Church-approved miracle. I do promise, however, that they are all true, and I hope that they stir your heart to desire to wear a blessed Miraculous Medal. For instance, there's the story of a young man behind the gelato counter in Rome, who was rubbing his shoulder in between filling gelato orders. It was at the Caffe Giolitti, a famous gelateria in Rome, not far from the Pantheon. I was in Rome attending a journalist's conference in September 2010. One evening after classes, a group of us headed to the gelateria.

I paid the cashier in advance for my mouth-watering delicacy and walked over to the counter, where I met up with countless others waiting for their dessert. When it came my time to be served, I told the young man the flavors I desired, but I asked him to catch his breath and take his time doing my order. I could see that his was a fast-paced job. I wasn't in a hurry; although this wasn't the case for the others around me pressing in line by the glass case, waiting for their famous, refreshing gelato.

As he filled my order, I asked him if his shoulder was hurting. He responded affirmatively. No doubt the swift pace required at the counter in that popular establishment caused the twinges of pain and the grimaces on his face. I kissed a Miraculous Medal, reached across the counter, and offered it to him. He smiled, took the medal from my hand, kissed it, and dropped it into his shirt pocket. I told him to wear it and that Mother Mary would help him. I hope he does wear it, and I trust that Mother Mary is working in his life.

A woman I met in a quick encounter at an airport became the very happy recipient of a blessed Miraculous Medal I had in my pocket that day. She thanked me profusely. Although we parted company hurriedly to make our flights, I was touched by her gratitude, and I hope the medal has continued to bless her life.

One time when I was giving a presentation on Long Island, New York, a woman named Patrice came up to me while I was standing at the podium a short while before I was going to speak. She told me that she would be buying a few of my books to evangelize her family. She then asked me for prayers for two family members—one on each side of the family—because they each had a brain tumor. I promised my prayers, reached into my pocket, and took out three blessed Miraculous Medals. These three had been from the batch

I had placed on John Paul II's tomb and Mother Teresa's bed. I kissed them, touched them to the one I was wearing, which Mother Teresa had given me, and handed them to Patrice, telling her that one was for her and one was for each of her relatives suffering from the brain tumors. I rarely have three medals in my pocket. I just providentially happened to that day, as my stash of medals was in another room on my book table.

One summer day, as I strolled along the sidewalk of a main street in the small, New England town of Northampton, Massachusetts, I came upon two fellows sitting on the edge of the sidewalk, their feet on the side of the street. The younger one, who seemed to be in his twenties, looked up at me as I passed by. He asked if I had any money to spare and quickly added, "We are both alcoholics. But at least we're honest ones." I told them that I was fairly sure that I didn't have any cash on me, but I might have about fifteen cents for them. They told me that they would be happy to receive my meager offering. I said I wanted to walk a bit further and would be back. As I walked up the sidewalk, I rummaged through my purse to find two blessed Miraculous Medals for them and a bit of loose change. Turning around, I headed back toward the two self-professed alcoholics and handed each of them a dime and a nickel. Then I kissed the two medals and told the men, "Here. This is something far more valuable than money. Wear the blessed Miraculous Medal and pray to the Blessed Mother." The younger of the two kissed the medal I offered him, thanked me, and dropped it into his shirt pocket. The older fellow thanked me, too.

Another story was told to me by my friend Mary, who said that the Miraculous Medal made a profound impact on her one day. She shared, "One night while working in the ICU, one of the chaplains who is a nun came to visit a sick patient and family. She pinned a Miraculous Medal on the bed. That loving gesture helped me understand that my work was my mission and not just my job. It had a profound impact on me because I remember that night after all these years."

Mary Convinced Her Faithful Servant

One time while I was attending a retreat given by Father John A. Hardon, S.J., my former spiritual director, now "Servant of God," Father told an amazing story to a captivated audience. He began by telling us that he previously was not the "medal-wearing kind of person." But witnessing a dramatic occurrence changed that. In fact, Father Hardon said the incident was "one of the most memorable experiences" he ever had.

I was literally on the edge of my seat, leaning in, waiting to find out what could have been so transforming. Father Hardon explained that when he was a young priest, in the fall of 1948, a visiting Vincentian priest paid a visit to the young Jesuit priests. The Vincentian recommended that they all enroll in the Confraternity of the Miraculous Medal. He told them, "Fathers, the medal works." He continued, "Miracles have been performed by Our Lady through the Miraculous Medal."

Father Hardon didn't think much of the message. It just didn't appeal to him; he didn't even own a Miraculous Medal. He said, "I was not impressed by what the Vincentian priest was telling." He ended up enrolling anyway, since it didn't cost him anything except the few minutes to fill out the form and the cost of a stamp to send it in. After a couple weeks, he received a Miraculous Medal leaflet of prayers from the confraternity and placed it in his Divine Office prayer book. Then he forgot about it.

A few months later, Father Hardon was assigned to help the chaplain at St. Alexis Hospital in Cleveland, Ohio, where countless Catholics were admitted regularly. Each day that he was there, Father Hardon did his best to visit as many as he could. One day during his rounds, Father Hardon came upon a young boy who was deep in a coma ten days after a sledding accident. It was a hopeless situation: The nine-year-old's skull was fractured, and he suffered from severe, inoperable, and permanent brain damage. Father Hardon felt that his job there was simply to try to console the distressed parents by speaking with them and giving the boy his blessing.

Suddenly, as Father was about to leave the room, an insistent thought came to him. He remembered the Vincentian priest's words from several months before. "The Miraculous Medal works." Father Hardon immediately thought he should test out the Miraculous Medal's powers. It couldn't hurt.

But a Miraculous Medal could not be found. Finally, one was acquired through the nursing sisters of the hospital. Because the Blessed Mother specifically instructed that the medal should be worn around the neck in order to receive great graces, a search was made for some type of necklace or chain.

At last a blue ribbon was found. Father said the blue ribbon made him feel silly: "What was I doing with medals and blue ribbons?" Father Hardon blessed the medal and asked the boy's father to hold up the leaflet that Father Hardon had received from the Vincentian priest so that Father could read the prayers of investiture. "No sooner did I finish the prayer of enrolling the boy in the Confraternity of the Miraculous Medal than he opened his eyes for the first time in almost two weeks. He saw his mother and said, 'Ma, I want some ice cream.'"

Everyone in the room was amazed beyond belief. They had witnessed a real miracle. The doctor was called immediately, and after checking the boy out, he allowed him to eat. Following a series of several thorough tests over the next three days, it was determined that the boy was completely cured of all brain damage. He was able to go home with his ecstatic and thankful parents.

From that day forward, for the rest of his life, Father Hardon wholeheartedly promoted the Miraculous Medal and the wonders that the Blessed Mother performs through it. Father Hardon told me that his life was dramatically changed because of this. He said, "This experience so changed my life that I have not been the same since. My faith in God, faith in His power to work miracles, was strengthened beyond description." He emphasized, "The wonders the Blessed Mother performs, provided we believe, are extraordinary."

A Parents' Gift of Devotion and Protection

My friend Theresa shared with me that her husband, Nelson, gave her a blessed Miraculous Medal early on in their marriage. He always wore one as well. It became a beloved tradition for the couple to give each of their five children a blessed Miraculous Medal, usually on the day of their first Holy Communion. Theresa is delighted when she gets a glimpse of her adult children wearing the medals still. She said, "After all these years, they're still wearing their medals!"

After Nelson's passing, Theresa continues to keep up the tradition of gifting Miraculous Medals to family members. All ten of her grandchildren wear the Miraculous Medal. Theresa assures me that as soon as the great grandchildren are old enough to wear the medals safely, she will be sure that each of them will have a Miraculous Medal, too. In addition to looking after her family members spiritually by providing them with blessed Miraculous Medals to wear, Theresa without fail prays the special Act of Consecration to Our Lady of the Miraculous Medal prayer each day for all in her family who are wearing the medal. I suspect Mother Mary is smiling lovingly down on Theresa.

Peace Overshadowed Her

Just before Christmas 2011, Wenqi and Craig Glantz were overjoyed to find out that they were expecting their second child. They chose names immediately—Lily if their baby was a girl, or Elijah if it was a boy. As Wenqi's twenty-week gestation date approached, she and Craig talked about their shared eagerness to find out their baby's gender.

Finally, on March 29, 2012, right before Holy Week, Craig and Wenqi waited patiently at the ultrasound appointment to learn more about their baby, finding out that it was a girl. The ultrasound technician, however, had some difficulty scanning their baby's head and explained that perhaps the baby was in an awkward position. So, she called for the doctor to assist her. The doctor scanned for nearly half an hour, totally engrossed in his work, not uttering a single word as he moved the probe back and forth over Wenqi's abdomen.

When he finished the exam, he delivered an unexpected diagnosis to the now-concerned couple. Their baby had anencephaly. The doctor explained that anencephaly is a condition that prevents the normal development of a baby's brain and the bones of the skull. An estimated one in one thousand pregnancies is affected by anencephaly, but most of these pregnancies end in miscarriage. The frequency of babies born with this condition is low: One in ten thousand infants in the United States is born with anencephaly.

The doctor recommended that Wenqi and Craig immediately abort their baby to terminate the pregnancy. Not expecting such shocking news, Wenqi and Craig overcame their surprise and in very clear terms told the doctor that abortion was absolutely not an option for them. They would carry their baby girl to full term, whenever that would be. God would decide when it would be, not them. They wanted to give Lily the fighting chance that she deserved—that every baby deserves. They said they were determined to "give her all the love" they possibly could.

Wenqi and Craig couldn't hold back their sobbing on the way home from the hospital. Through their tears, they decided to give their little Lily the middle name Gianna, after the Italian saint Gianna Beretta Molla, who hero-ically sacrificed her own life for the sake of her unborn baby. Craig and Wenqi daily prayed to St. Gianna and many other saints, begging for their interces-sion for a miraculous full healing of Lily Gianna. After requesting prayers from their Catholic community of friends, prayers poured in and heaven was stormed for good health for the baby.

When I heard that Wenqi and Craig's unborn baby had been diagnosed with anencephaly, I prayed fervently for a miracle and hoped that maybe the doctor was wrong. I felt compelled to send two blessed Miraculous Medals to them. These were ones that I had placed on Pope John Paul II's tomb and Mother Teresa's bed.

Wenqi wore one of the blessed Miraculous Medals I had sent during the remaining four months of her pregnancy. Before receiving the medal from me, she had always worn the Miraculous Medal given to her by Craig during their engagement. She now wore both!

Many times throughout her pregnancy, Wenqi visited the Miraculous Medal Shrine in Germantown, Pennsylvania. On Monday July 30, 2012, the last day of work before Wenqi's maternity leave would start, and about two weeks before Lily's due date, she drove over to the shrine once again.

Wenqi made a good confession and participated in the Miraculous Medal novena that was held at the shrine. Somehow she sensed that this visit might be her last before Lily's arrival into the world. Kneeling in front of the statue of the Blessed Mother, Wenqi pleaded for a full healing of her precious baby girl, just as she did each Monday when she visited the shrine, but perhaps this time with more intensity since Lily's birth was drawing near. Wenqi knelt a long while before the image of Our Lady of the Miraculous Medal. She explained to me later her experience:

> Immersed in deep prayers, I opened my eyes to the opening arms
> of Our Lady, her loving gesture inviting me: "Let go, my dear child,
> let go of your little Lily to me." I then looked up at the ceiling of
> the chapel. I noticed there for the first time the drawings of the
> many saints, holy and loving, a company of peace, love, and joy. A
> thought was brought to my mind: If Lily is going to be in the loving
> care and presence of our Blessed Mother and all these holy men and
> women, I will let Lily go. Tears welled up in my eyes; a tremendous
> sense of peace overshadowed me. For the first time in the last four
> months (ever since we found out that Lily had anencephaly), I felt a
> sense of relief. Perhaps that is the true letting go process.

The faith of Wenqi and Craig brought them an abiding hope. As Lily Gianna's due date approached, they continually prayed for a safe delivery and never gave up hoping for a miraculous healing. Lily Gianna's day of birth came sooner than was expected. Just two days after Wenqi let go of her baby, entrusting her to Our Lady of the Miraculous Medal, on August 1, she began having a few contractions. Craig and Wenqi set out for morning Mass, and during Mass the contractions increased and grew stronger.

At 3:00 P.M., the "Hour of Great Mercy" according to the Divine Mercy devotion, Wenqi was admitted to the hospital and monitored by doctors and nurses. Craig created a small shrine in the delivery room consisting of the Miraculous Medal, pictures of the Sacred Heart of Jesus and the Immaculate Heart of Mary, and various sacramentals and holy cards.

At 5:10 P.M., without any difficulty or complications, Lily Gianna emerged into the world to the delight of her parents. Wenqi and Craig attributed their baby's safe delivery to the intercession of Mother Mary and the countless prayers being offered for the family.

Graces abounded. "The moment when Lily emerged into the world, we didn't even care about whether she had anencephaly or not," Wenqi told me. Craig expressed, "Seeing Lily safely arrive was a huge relief to us. She had a heartbeat, and we were more relieved and excited than we had imagined!"

They felt tremendous peace when Lily arrived. Craig explained, "Everything was very peaceful and quite calm. At that moment, we were not even disappointed that the miracle of full healing did not happen. We were just excited that Lily was alive." Wenqi added, "The fact that she was alive and Craig was able to baptize her immediately was a miracle to us."

For the next hour and eighteen minutes, Wenqi and Craig lovingly cradled Lily Gianna and covered her with kisses and caresses. At 6:28 P.M. their baby girl passed on into eternal life. "We were both swept by a tremendous sense of peace," Craig expressed. "We knew our good Lord had just taken Lily home, the eternal home we all long for. Lily now has joined the many angels and saints, rejoicing in heaven, smiling down upon us, interceding for our prayer intentions."

Seeking Mother Mary's Intercession

Mother Teresa, whom I was blessed to know, had a beautiful and close relationship with the Blessed Mother. As I mentioned earlier, she gave a blessed Miraculous Medal to many of the people she met—sharing tens of thousands of medals. She also prayed the rosary constantly as well as the Memorare prayer to the Blessed Mother. She kept prayerful company with Mary.

I heard about the time in the early seventies when Mother Teresa wanted to purchase a dwelling for the Missionaries of Charity in Dublin, Ireland. The price was higher than she could afford, so as Mother Teresa left the property, she tossed a blessed Miraculous Medal into the garden. An unexpected monetary donation came in soon afterward, which would be almost enough to buy the property. On the same day, the real-estate agent called Mother Teresa to tell her that the owners of the property had expressed that they would sell the property to Mother Teresa cheaper than they had advertised so that the sisters could turn it into a house full of love. Mother Teresa had the exact amount of money from the donation to purchase the property.

A priest I met named Father Matthew told me about the time he was assisting Mother Teresa. While they were in St. Louis, Missouri, they tossed many Miraculous Medals on various properties. He told me he thought it was kind of funny and didn't have a clear idea why they were doing this but he went along with it and came to realize that Mother Teresa knew what she was doing!

Mother Teresa would many times ask a sick person, "Where does it hurt?" She would gently rub a blessed Miraculous Medal on an area of the body of someone who was suffering in some way. Completely trusting in the intercession of the Blessed Mother, she would say, "Let Our Lady kiss where it hurts."

Even just a few short months before she died, Mother Teresa was still distributing blessed Miraculous Medals. During her last visit to a convent in the South Bronx, New York, she sat in a wheelchair, handing out countless medals to priests and laity. She kissed the medals before passing them on and suggested they be used to evangelize—to spread the Gospel message of love.

RESUSCITATED TWENTY-EIGHT TIMES

One day I received an e-mail from a woman who had heard me speak at a women's conference in Boston, Massachusetts. I had met her afterward at my book table, where I was giving out blessed Miraculous Medals to all who came to meet me there. Bridget had asked me for a few extra medals because she wanted to give them to her husband and children.

In her e-mail, she said: "Writing to let you know that we just had a miracle happen. My husband had a massive heart attack and cardiac arrest at the same time. They had to revive him twenty-eight times." Her e-mail immediately caught my attention.

Bridget told me that she and her husband, Bob O'Shaughnessy, were out on their daily walk when Bob felt uncharacteristically weak and had to sit down on a nearby bench. Soon after, Bob went into cardiac arrest, and she called an ambulance. He was taken straight to the emergency room. En route, his heart stopped over twenty times, and he had to be resuscitated each time.

Unfortunately, the heart attack was not Bob's only problem. An artery supplying blood to Bob's heart was completely blocked. At the hospital, doctors immediately worked on his heart to restore the blood flow, but during the emergency balloon angioplasty, Bob's heart stopped again. Bridget wrote, "They inserted a stent within two hours. He was then placed in a medically induced coma for over two weeks. There were several complications along the way, like needing blood transfusions, getting an infection, getting pneumonia, and more."

Bob was transferred to a nearby tertiary hospital, which was equipped to perform a heart transplant if needed. He remained in the medically induced coma while being treated for his life-threatening conditions. When Bob was finally discharged from the hospital, he was remarkably in outstanding cardiovascular health.

Bridget added that despite all of the odds against her husband, he was doing really well. "Doctors had no hope for him. It was minute to minute for days on end," she recounted to me. Both Bridget and Bob attribute the astonishing and miraculous recovery to Our Lady's intercession through a blessed Miraculous Medal. Bridget said, "We are so thankful since he was carrying in his wallet the Miraculous Medal that I got from you at the Catholic women's conference in Boston back in February of this year. I was the one that asked for extra medals for my family, and you were kind enough to give them to me." Bridget would later tell me that her husband couldn't wear the medal because of a skin condition, but he had faithfully kept it with him along with his Celtic cross, tucked away in his wallet.

Bridget was not only writing that day to tell me about her husband's miracle but to ask for additional blessed medals. She wanted at least fifty. She said, "I can give them to my friends and family who supported our family through this since there are a lot of people that witnessed this." Bridget wanted to thank them in a special way by passing on what she believed was the conduit of graces that saved her husband. She wanted the doctors, nurses, paramedics, technicians, friends, and family members to be able to experience graces through the medals in whatever way the Lord intended for them, too. I was so happy to oblige Bridget to help spread the Miraculous Medal devotion further.

The Baby Who Died Three Times

A woman I met at my speaking event in New Jersey shared a beautiful story with me about her son Tim. Margie had two daughters and a son when she found out she was pregnant again. Instead of rejoicing, she cried. She was Rh-positive and knew that there was a potential for serious problems with her pregnancies. She was told she should abort her baby.

Instead, Margie prayed very hard that God would help her adjust to the pregnancy and be happy about it. After a while, she began to feel better emotionally. When she was beginning her sixth month of pregnancy, Margie was sent to see the New York doctor who invented the RhoGAM shot. He checked on Margie's amniotic fluid every week to be sure that Margie's blood wasn't affecting her unborn baby. But because of the amniocentesis procedures, Margie started leaking fluid and was told to get off her feet as much as possible.

One day Margie walked to a "Right to Life" Mass with her children. During the Mass, Margie was overcome with stabbing pains. She cried and prayed, feeling worried that she would lose the baby, whom she didn't want at first but was so in love with now. As soon as she returned home, she got into bed and prayed. During her rosary, she started bleeding and had to be taken to Columbia Presbyterian Hospital in New York, where she was monitored closely. Her husband stayed with her as long as he could but eventually had to leave to care for the other children. Margie felt totally alone, knowing that she would most likely have to go through the delivery without him.

Margie felt that she was having full-blown contractions, but the hospital staff didn't seem to think so. It was three months before her due date. Margie continued to pray, "Lord please help me. Mary, please help me."

She was transferred to the delivery room and given oxygen. The residents were chatting among themselves. One of them said, "Okay, now how are we going to get this baby out?" Margie told me, "I ripped the mask off and said that I would push him out; they had to do everything possible and have everything ready for the baby."

"Lady, this baby is not going to make it. It is too early."

Margie told them to do their job and be sure to have someone ready to take care of the baby.

Shortly afterward, Tim was born. Margie thought she heard a faint cry, but she was told he wasn't breathing. Margie was whisked away into a room where she waited with other mothers. They were eager to see their new babies. She said to me later, "I was the only one there whose baby was dead."

She called her husband and priest friend. They both arrived at the hospital about the same time. "As I told them that Tim was dead, the nurse came in and said that he was alive—barely." Tim weighed in at two pounds and four ounces.

Margie was allowed to see him ever so briefly. He was covered with wires and tubes, and he was on a ventilator. The doctor told her that Tim wouldn't make it. Then Margie was sent upstairs to rest. She prayed, "Dear Jesus, dear Mary, please help my poor little guy."

Prayers were unceasing, and Margie pinned a tiny Miraculous Medal to Tim's clothing. In the next seventy-seven days, Tim died three times. He had bleeding on the brain. He had surgery on his tiny heart. Margie and her husband were told constantly that Tim would probably not make it, and if he did, "he would be a vegetable," unable to walk, talk, eat, sit, smile, or to do anything a normal child could.

The third time bringing Tim back to life was difficult. The doctors asked the parents if they wanted to keep reviving him. Did they want him to live on a respirator for the rest of his life? Margie and her husband prayed long and hard, begging Jesus and Mary to tell them what to do. They told the doctors to do everything possible for him but not to put him on a respirator or ventilator again. Margie asked them to wean him off the respirator very slowly so that he could adjust and to make sure he was being fed well to strengthen him.

After ten days of weaning, the doctor said, "Now you have to live with the fact that he is going to live. What are you going to do with him? He should be institutionalized."

Many of the tests showed much brain damage, and Tim's eyes had been injured from too much oxygen so that he was almost blind. He only had one tenth of a cerebellum, which is the motor of the brain. Again and again, Margie was reminded that her son would not be able to do anything, that he would be a vegetable. Margie decided to see that for herself and raise Tim as if he would be able to function.

Margie's friend Father John brought the Blessed Sacrament in and touched the host to Tim's tiny tongue. Another priest friend came in and blessed Tim with holy water from Lourdes and prayed to "Mary, Help of Christians." As the prayer was recited and Tim was blessed with the Lourdes water while Margie was holding him, a warmth went through Margie. The next day, the doctors said the damage in Tim's eyes had diminished dramatically. Margie sought reassurance that she would have "something to develop" in Tim. She prayed to the Blessed Mother asking her to remember Jesus's first smile and to please help little Tim to smile. Two days later on a Sunday morning, Tim smiled for the first time at five months old.

Tim grew up with some health problems but was a happy and loving boy. His mother raised him with great patience and love and praised him for all of his accomplishments. When Tim was five years old, his grandfather was dying, and Tim comforted him. After he died, Tim began to wear his grandfather's Miraculous Medal. Tim never took it off. He always felt very close to Mary and would love to sing the Hail Mary.

Before Tim's fifth open-heart surgery, when he was thirty years old, he felt anxious and worried that he would die. He clung to his Miraculous Medal. As he was being wheeled into surgery, he kept wearing it until the last possible moment before going into the operating room and then handed it off to his mother.

"Only then did he let them take it off, and I gave it back to him as soon as he came out of surgery, though it was hard to wear with his scar, but it was always near him or hanging down in back," his mother reported. He's been wearing that medal now for thirty years.

Tim, now thirty-five years old, is an amazing young man who is very kind and caring and loved by everyone. He is neurologically impaired but works with special-needs children, preparing horses and their tack for the children's hippotherapy.

A Parent's Nightmare: A Daughter's Addiction

My friend (I'll call her Sophie) shared with me about her daughter's scary diagnosis of a brain cyst and her struggles with substance abuse. The Miraculous Medal was a comfort and blessing to her family during this difficult time, and her family's faith was strengthened through their prayers and help received from the Blessed Mother.

While at a relative's home celebrating Thanksgiving, Sophie's daughter Susan had a full-blown seizure for the first time ever. The celebration abruptly ended because Susan had to go to the hospital, where many medical tests were administered. The doctors couldn't figure out what was wrong, because the tests were inconclusive.

Since Sophie and her husband had previously suspected that their daughter might have a drinking problem, they had broached the subject with her before Thanksgiving. Susan admitted to having issues with alcohol and pain-medication abuse. They were planning to seek help right after Thanksgiving, and then the seizure happened, stopping them all in their tracks and forcing them to react.

Sophie poured her motherly heart out to Mother Mary, praying through the Miraculous Medal and the rosary. Her husband joined her in prayer, and together they sought Mother Teresa's intercession as well.

They made a visit to their family physician, where Susan disclosed the addiction troubles she endured. The family doctor sent her to a neurologist, who ended up not charging for three visits since Susan's health insurance wasn't accepted by his practice. He ordered an MRI of Susan's brain, which revealed a pineal cyst there.

When Sophie told me that her daughter was suffering from bad headaches and a brain cyst, I gave her a blessed Miraculous Medal for her to wear. It was one that I had placed on John Paul II's tomb and Mother Teresa's bed. Sophie told me that she wore it and that many wonderful things started to happen.

The seizure was a blessing in disguise, since through it they had found the cyst. The doctor said it was probably benign, but he decided they would keep an eye on it to be sure. He said it would probably not grow larger or affect any part of her brain. The neurologist concluded that the seizure (and two more episodes she had after the first scare) was from a dip in alcohol consumption. Susan had been trying hard secretly on her own to rid herself of her alcohol and drug addictions.

Susan's mother and father worked with her to get her all the help she needed and bolstered it with prayer support. Sophie went to every appointment with her daughter. A few close people were privy to the situation and prayed as well.

Sophie is convinced of the power of prayer and the amazing graces attached to the Miraculous Medal. She told me, "With all of us praying so hard—she was also wearing the Miraculous Medal during her recovery as were we—wonderful events started to happen for her." Sophie was pleasantly surprised at how everything unfolded, and this affirmed her beliefs. "Opportunities opened up just at the right moments continuously for her. Many strong people have been put in her life, just at the right moments. Most all of these individuals have a strong faith and belief in God and Mary," she expressed. Sophie knew prayer was necessary because, as she said, "Susan needed to be strong through all of this and she was given this strength. None of these events are believed by us or Susan to be coincidence."

Susan had always worn the Miraculous Medal since she was a young girl, but at times she temporarily lost one. Sophie, as a protective mother, would give Susan her own medal to wear right away and would get a new one blessed for herself. "Always, these lost Miraculous Medals would come back to her. Today, she is wearing more than one Miraculous Medal around her neck," Sophie recalled about Susan.

Sophie shared happily that Susan "thanks God and Mary for giving her this challenge and insight in her recovery and the strength to get through it. She strongly believes everything happens for a reason." Susan has made plans for the future based on her experience. "She would like to move forward using her social-work degree, helping and counseling others in their life struggles in recovery," Sophie said. "Susan strongly believes that she is where she is today, which is clean and sober, only by the grace of God and the help of her beloved Mary and all the prayers said for her."

A Wife's Deepest Prayer: Believing Without Seeing

My friend Linda told me, "When I married my husband many years ago, he was Catholic, but was not a practicing Catholic. He believed in God but this is where it ended." Gary felt he had no reason to go to Mass because he believed that everything had a good, sensible, even scientific reason behind it. He believed "miracles" had nothing to do with God or Mary. He found no reason to believe. From his perspective, if he did not see it with his own eyes, he did not believe it. "My family lovingly called him 'the scientist'" Linda told me.

"I prayed to Mary through the rosary and the Miraculous Medal to help me to bring my husband into the Church," she said. She prayed constantly to both Jesus and Mary, asking that they "help soften him and his beliefs."

One can't force another to believe in God, and Linda knew this. Still, she didn't give up on faithfully praying for a dramatic change to occur in her husband. In the Gospel of Mark we read about blind Bartimaeus, who cried out to Jesus to have pity on him. People nearby tried to quiet the man, but Bartimaeus persisted. When Jesus asked him, "What do you want me to do for you?" the blind man said, "Master, let me receive my sight" (Mark 10:51). And Jesus healed the man's blindness, telling him that it was because of his faith that he was healed. We all have a deep inner longing to see—to see with the eyes of faith. Sophie gave the situation of her husband's "blindness" to God, trusting him and the Blessed Mother with her innermost desires for Gary to believe and to come into the graces of the Church.

Linda's faith and persistence (like that of Bartimaeus) paid off in an incredible way. "My prayers were answered…when my husband one day said to me that he was going to come with the children and me to Mass." Right after that Mass with the family, Gary made many positive strides toward the faith, including getting involved in the parish Rite of Christian Initiation of Adults (RCIA) program. Through it, he made his sacraments of first reconciliation, first Communion, and confirmation. Our Lord and his Blessed Mother were working mightily on Gary, for after he completed the program, he desired to help others come into the Church and began assisting with RCIA.

Linda couldn't be happier. Gary had learned to believe without seeing. She shared, "My husband is no longer known as 'the scientist' by my family, and he firmly believes without *seeing* for himself that Mary, Jesus, and the Holy Spirit really do exist and help him through his everyday journey through life." She added, "My husband also makes sure he is wearing the Miraculous Medal every day. Thank you once again to Our Lady, Father, Son, and Holy Spirit."

Wine Store Owner Celebrates a New Birthday

One summer afternoon I visited a favorite little wine store in my town. It's a charming store with a festive atmosphere featuring a nice variety of wines and a smattering of unique gifts, too. But this particular day, the upbeat ambiance seemed lacking—completely. In its place was a gloomy tone. Dolly, one of the owners, appeared especially distraught. I asked her how she was doing, and she blurted it all out, shedding a few tears in the process. She explained that her husband, Jeffrey (the other store owner), was in immediate need of a new aortic heart valve because his was found to be failing quickly. He had to wait and get through a series of important tests, though, which made Dolly beyond terrified because of the pressure for time and the severity of the situation.

Their discovery of Jeff's dire need for a heart operation came about in a strange way. Jeffrey, being a Vietnam veteran, was encouraged by another veteran to get checked for his medical needs because he was now sixty-five years old, and in some cases, veterans at that age could have the services paid for. So, Jeff went in for a physical about an hour's ride from the wine store. He told the doctor about his recent shortness of breath and fatigue, which he attributed to working long hours six days a week. He had the feeling that something was wrong "but didn't know it was that dire," he said. His wife, Dolly, got the phone call a short time later. Jeff told her that he was given a bottle of nitroglycerin and only one month to live. The doctor had informed Jeff that his aortic valve was failing quickly and needed to be replaced. In addition, at the stage that Jeff was at, the surgery would have only a one-in-three survival rate. This was an equation Jeff knew all too well. When he was a chief gunner on dangerous missions in enemy territory in Vietnam, using an M60 machine gun while flying helicopter gunships, only one in three survived.

Jeff's motto became, "To it and through it." He said, "Every minute was touch and go." He wanted to make it to his surgery and hoped and prayed to get through it.

Dolly said, "I know, being raised a Catholic, that God wants us to pray, but I always think God is so busy that I only leave messages for him at the most serious times. So, I left three messages." The first time Dolly left God a message was when riding home after signing the consent forms. "I prayed he would please keep him alive until August 15," because that was the day he'd have his operation.

When Jeff was having tests administered in preparation for the surgery, the doctor had taken Dolly aside and informed her "he could go any minute doing the smallest of tasks." Dolly was petrified. "We only have each other and I felt like I was dying, as well," she told me.

The day I stopped in the wine shop and heard Dolly's story, I pulled out a blessed Miraculous Medal and told Dolly that it was very special and that many graces were associated with it. I wanted her to give it to her husband, and I prayed he would accept it and maybe even wear it. I told Dolly that I had placed it on John Paul II's tomb and Mother Teresa's bed, and I told her of the power in the medal itself. I explained that it wasn't superstitious or a lucky charm but a sacramental of the Church, and it would give Jeff some comfort. I promised my prayers for them both.

Dolly observed, "The medal gave Jeff great hope and courage. He kept it in his pocket, and he would hold it for strength." Jeff later told me, "The medal certainly made a big difference, giving me another vote of confidence and good vibration." But a few days later he lost the medal. They were both upset and looked all over for it.

The next day, I felt an overwhelming need to stop by at the wine store. I had in my hand two blessed Miraculous Medals and didn't even know why I was bringing them two more. When I got out of my car, Dolly came out into the parking lot with an ecstatic look on her face. She later recalled, "I got chills when I saw her because she was bringing in another medal, knowing we needed it." I gave her the two blessed medals—one for each of them. Dolly was very appreciative and seemed to have tears in her eyes. I was just so happy that I had followed the sudden urge to stop by. Dolly later surmised, "I hadn't left a message then, but God and Mother Teresa must have been watching us for a while. I wore the medal and Jeff's wedding ring on a chain until Jeff was released from the hospital."

The day of the surgery arrived. Jeff had made it that far. It was August 15, and the surgery was scheduled for 7:30 A.M. Jeff said going in for the operation was "unnerving," but he had to do it; he had no other choice. "As I watched Jeff walk down the hall to the prep room, I prayed and cried my heart out," Dolly recalled. The surgery was difficult and prolonged. "Jeff's valve had failed on the table during surgery," Dolly shared. Instead of lasting for six to eight hours as initially estimated, the surgery took almost thirteen hours instead.

"I held that medal and his ring the whole time," Dolly told me. And the surgery was a success. "We are both eternally grateful for the kindness and care, not to mention the half-million-dollar surgery that was successful. Everyone at the West Haven, Connecticut, veterans hospital was amazed, and we were blessed to have them orchestrate our miracle." Dolly said her third message to God was "short and sweet. It was, 'Thank you!'"

Jeff is very thankful for the kindnesses and prayers of those who showed their support. He said, "I'm sure God put his hand in there from time to time." Jeff said sometimes he wakes up in the morning and thinks, "Wow, I'm here!"

When I visited the couple after Jeff had recovered from his valve-transplant surgery and was back at the store, both Dolly and Jeff shared with me that they consider his day of surgery to be "a second birthday" for Jeff. I reminded them that August 15 was a special day, the feast of the Assumption of the Blessed Virgin Mary, and that Mary had clearly watched over him!

Labor of Love Along with a Gift for a Peaceful Death

One time when sending out a book order, I felt inspired to include three blessed Miraculous Medals rather than only one as I normally do. The woman, Julie, who ordered the books was very happy to receive them and shared an amazing story about one of the medals with me a short time later.

A woman in Julie's parish was just home from the hospital, recuperating from an amputation surgery. Parishioners had arranged for hot meals to be delivered to Anne's home to help her and her family in their time of need. Julie volunteered to make a homemade hot meal for her.

On the way to deliver the home-cooked meal, Julie was struck with an inspiration. She had a strong feeling that she should turn around, go back home, and get one of the blessed Miraculous Medals I had sent to her. She would give it to the woman along with the meal.

So, she went home to get the blessed Medal and then headed back out and delivered the meal. It wasn't without difficulty, because her young children were extra rambunctious that day. Despite the challenges, Julie wanted to fulfill her promise. Anne's family was very appreciative of the meal, the blessed medal, and Julie's kind words when delivering them to the family.

The next morning, Julie dropped her daughter off at school and went over to morning Mass. She thought she misheard the monsignor when he announced to the congregation that they'd be praying for Anne because she had passed away that morning. But Julie had heard correctly. As sad as she was, she felt relieved that she had followed through by bringing the meal to Anne's family and giving Anne the blessed Miraculous Medal. She hoped that the medal had made Anne's death a more peaceful experience for her and her family.

Obstacles Shrouded in Grace

Jeanne had been diagnosed with a dreaded infertility disease, polycystic ovary syndrome. But seven years into her marriage, Jeanne felt very blessed by a miracle: amazingly, she was pregnant!

During her pregnancy, she had a deep relationship with Mary, the Mother of God. "I grew close to the Blessed Mother. I learned to love the rosary and to trust in her motherly protection," Jeanne shared.

"At twenty-four weeks I went into pre-labor," Jeanne explained. "I was three centimeters dilated, 80 percent effaced, and the doctor, who lacked any semblance of compassion, coldly told me that our first child would be born too early and would probably be disabled." Jeanne chose to pray and hope instead. "I held my rosary and prayed, and my friends and family prayed," she said.

Jeanne's condition was stabilized, but she had to commit herself to three months of complete bed rest and was so happy to make it to just about thirty-seven weeks gestation. Then, on November 13, 1988, Jonathan was born weighing seven pounds and one ounce. The proud mama said, "Yes, every ounce counts when you have a preemie, and for us, he was a miracle."

The overjoyed couple rejoiced in their miracle baby. But soon afterward a new challenge came upon them. They were told that Jonathan had a bubble in his lungs that might require surgery. His parents looked on him in his incubator with heavy hearts. There were many wires attached to little Jonathan.

Jonathan was promptly baptized. Jeanne hung images of Mother Mary and the Sacred Heart of Jesus on Jonathan's little abode. The holy reminders helped them to focus on God's will. The many wires were troubling Jonathan's father, Paul, who wished he could remove them and take his sweet baby home. Jeanne reminded her husband that they needed to pray and trust God. "He didn't bring us this far to abandon us," she reassured Paul.

Jeanne still smiles when she recalls what happened next. The following morning, the nurse came into the room laughing and told them that that during the night Jonathan had thrashed around and had ripped all of his monitors and oxygen out. His vital signs and breathing were normal, and there was no more need for surgery! Jeanne said, "The nurse said all he needed was a good cry and his lungs were fine." One reason Jeanne smiles about this is "because to this day he is very verbal."

Before long, little Jonathan was able to go to his new home with his happy parents, just in time for a Thanksgiving celebration. Jeanne went to her follow-up OB-GYN appointment and was shocked to be told that she had a large cyst on her ovary that might need to be surgically removed. She was told to stop nursing Jonathan and to take birth control pills, and she would be assessed for surgery. An ultrasound was scheduled for that same week.

"This was news I did not want to hear. I was a new mother intent on nursing my newborn son, who, being born three weeks early, required the very best a mother could give him," Jeanne expressed. She immediately turned to the Blessed Mother. She began to attend the weekly Miraculous Medal novena at her local parish. "I told Our Lady that I trusted her to take care of this for us." In the past when Jeanne had attended the novena, she didn't ask for anything in particular, just for the faith she needed to follow God's will. But now she trusted that Our Lady of the Miraculous Medal would help them in this trial. "I knew for Jonathan's sake I had to ask for help so I could nurse him and avoid surgery. I left there feeling comforted by her prayers, not knowing anything except that she understood and would pray for us," she said. Jeanne added, "I believed the Blessed Mother wanted the best for Jonathan, or so many graces would not have been given to him and our family."

The day arrived for Jeanne's appointment with the ultrasound specialist. "The technician was quiet at first and then asked questions about my previous appointment. She then announced that she could not find a cyst anywhere. She asked me if I felt any pain recently, sharp and sudden." Jeanne told the technician that she hadn't felt any pain whatsoever. The ultrasound technician explained that if the cyst were the type that would erupt, she would be able to see its remains on the uterus during the ultrasound exam, but she had found no sign of it. She could not offer an explanation—she was baffled. Jeanne asked if the doctor could have been mistaken. The technician said it couldn't have been a mistake because of the size of the cyst that the doctor diagnosed.

Two years later, Jonathan's sister Christine was born. Four years after Christine had blessed their lives, Maria came along. Later on, at twelve weeks, Joseph Marie was lost to miscarriage. Through their loss, the Blessed Mother comforted Jeanne and her husband.

Now twenty-four years after Jonathon was born, his parents are still counting their blessings that their son is not disabled like the doctor had predicted. In fact, he had a perfect verbal score on his SAT test and is a talented pianist. Jeanne and Paul feel thoroughly blessed to have been gifted with all their children.

Near His Heart, Right Along with His Dog Tags

When traveling in Texas and waiting for my next flight at the Dallas airport, I happened to sit down next to an army officer dressed in his fatigues. I felt an urge to speak to him, so I simply said, "Hello." He told me that he was coming back from Afghanistan for a week reprieve and would be very happy to see his wife and family. We chatted for a while. He told me that he had been in the service for about thirty-nine years. His father and his brother were military pilots and had often suggested that he, too, study to become a pilot. But this serviceman didn't want any part of flying, he said. Yet, as he shared his story he chuckled at the sheer irony that his work in the military meant constant flights for him.

I felt inspired to offer this man two blessed Miraculous Medals, one for his wife and one for him. I was so pleased that he accepted them. And even better, he reached behind his neck to unclasp his chain, drew it in front of him, and added one of the medals right next to his dog tags. Wow. My heart was soaring. I thanked Jesus and Mary. I told him I would pray that he would be protected in all of his travels and he was immensely thankful.

My Sister's Journey Home to Heaven

When my sister Barbara called me from the intensive-care unit at her hospital, I knew that something was terribly wrong. She had been in remission for lung cancer but suddenly began experiencing a series of life-threatening symptoms and had been admitted to the hospital. She told me over the phone that day that the doctors suspected she was suffering from acute leukemia but couldn't be certain about her condition until the results from a battery of tests came back from the lab.

I promised Barbara my prayers, but I will admit I felt a bit helpless since I lived so far away from my sister. She was in Texas, and I was in Connecticut. I wanted to hug her. I wanted to make her healthy fruit smoothies. I wanted to make the cancer go away—somehow. I was beginning to believe that Barbara might not have much more time left here on earth. So, I made the decision to tie up loose ends with my family and my work and to jump on a plane and see her. Barbara was thrilled that I would be visiting. By the time I arrived in Texas, Barbara had been released from the hospital and was in hospice care at her home. It was wonderful to see her, although my heart was sorely aching to know that Barbara was indeed afflicted with acute leukemia and had been given a prognosis of only a few weeks to live.

The following day when things were a little quieter, I showed Barbara the blessed Miraculous Medal I brought for her. It was one of those that I had placed on John Paul II's tomb and Teresa's bed. Barbara asked me if I would place it on the chain she wore that held her cross. I kissed the medal, touched it to the one I wear, placed it on her chain, and helped her put it back around her neck.

A few short days later, my sister Barbara died peacefully at her home on July 27, the anniversary of St. Catherine Labouré's canonization (July 27, 1947). Barbara was about two-and-a half years old when St. Catherine Labouré was canonized on that day.

On a Pile of Dirt

Tony faithfully wears his Miraculous Medal every day. One summer when he was working with his cousin for a construction company, Tony sadly lost his Miraculous Medal. He noticed it was missing when he had already left the job site. His medal had fallen off the chain, which remained around his neck. Tony shared his disappointment with his mother that evening, telling her he would not know where to start looking on the property, because he was not sure where he had lost it. He felt that it might be lost for good since he had been doing a lot of digging in the dirt that day, and it possibly could be buried.

Tony and his coworkers would not be going back to the construction site (which was approximately an hour away from his home) for a while. His mother told him she would look for another Miraculous Medal for him. Approximately one month later, Tony returned to the property to continue working. When he and his coworkers arrived at the property, the owner came out of the house and walked up to Tony. A few other workers had arrived at the same time, but the owner singled out Tony, which he thought was strange because the question she was about to ask could have been directed to any one of the workers.

The owner asked Tony, "Did you lose a medallion?" She held it up to Tony, and it was his Miraculous Medal. Tony asked where she had found it, and she told him that she had been outside a couple of days after his crew had left (about a month earlier) and something caught her eye shining on the top of a dirt pile. She went over to see what was sparkling in the sun and found what she referred to as the medallion. She told Tony that she just thought it would have belonged to him. Needless to say, Tony was thrilled to get it back.

BREATHING A SIGH OF RELIEF

My friend Polly, a convert to Catholicism, had sensed the Blessed Mother in her life and had the desire to pray to her even before she was Catholic. This is pretty remarkable because Polly was raised a Baptist, and as she said, "The whole idea of Mary was a hurdle as it is with most Protestants."

Yet she shared, "My relationship with Mary has been growing since even before I became Catholic. I prayed the Hail Mary and the Memorare, and talked with Mary a lot about my issues and struggles with marriage, my past, my relationships, and my worries." Polly said, "I began to see her as my 'best woman friend' who had been through a lot herself and could sympathize with me and pray for me even when I didn't have a close woman friend on earth to share those things with."

Polly began listening to Catholic radio on the trip to and from work. One day she blurted out to her husband, "Well, I'm Catholic now!" She felt she had a conversion of heart. So, she immediately registered for the RCIA program, and after taking classes in the faith she was baptized a Catholic.

One day when I was chatting with Polly, I told her that I felt inspired to send her a blessed Miraculous Medal. She was very appreciative and looked forward to receiving it. A few months later, Polly shared a dilemma she had about the medal with me. She said she didn't wear it much at all. The issue may sound vain, she explained, but it boiled down to the fact that Polly didn't have a chain that she liked to wear it on. "One chain was too shiny, one was not special enough, and one had other charms and pendants on it. Nothing felt right!" she explained.

Her husband's need for surgery changed all of that. The night before Bob's hip replacement, Polly got her clothes ready for the next morning so she could save time, since they would be leaving for the hospital at the crack of dawn. She told me later, "I knew I wanted to wear the medal because I knew I would be feeling stressed and wanted to keep Our Mother close," Polly said. As she prepared for the next day, she spotted the crucifix she received when coming into the Church. It was a gift from her mother-in-law. "I slipped the Miraculous Medal onto the chain and it was like breathing a sigh of relief. This was where the medal belonged for me—next to Jesus. Mary always leads us to her Son."

She went on, "Wearing the necklace the next day, I was continually reminded of Our Mother's protection and care for us as her children, and of her Son's sacrifice for us, which was a great comfort during Bob's surgery."

Under Her Pillow

Julie and Chad rushed with their three young boys to the hospital to visit their ailing grandmother. Ruth had been suffering from Alzheimer's disease, which had been rapidly progressing. Just recently she had fallen and broken her hip, and now she was also suffering from kidney failure. The prognosis was grim. Julie and Chad were not merely concerned for Ruth's physical health but even more important, for her eternal salvation. They knew she was getting closer to her eternal reward, and they felt called to step in and act in some way—even beyond their rosaries and Divine Mercy chaplets they had been praying for Ruth for years—to help her to get to heaven. Ruth had always been supportive of the family's sacramental celebrations throughout the years, even though she herself had not ever been baptized.

At one point, Julie and Chad feared Ruth would die without the precious gift of baptism. They called for their priest, but he was unavailable. The decision was made for Chad to baptize his grandmother. Later on, arrangements were made for Ruth to receive the sacrament of the anointing of the sick. Since it was so close to Christmas, the three young boys gathered around Ruth's hospital bed and sang her a few heartwarming Christmas carols. Ruth opened her eyes wide during one song. At another time, she gripped one of the little boy's hands tightly and drew it close to her heart. She clearly appreciated their visits and the love they poured out for her.

One night by Ruth's bedside, Julie felt overcome with grace. "As I studied the crucifix in her hospital room late at night and was praying the rosary, and looking at Ruth's beautiful face, I absolutely, completely, truly saw Jesus," she recalled to me. "And as I kissed her face, I thought of kissing Jesus's face. I wondered if that's how Veronica felt when she lovingly and compassionately cared for Jesus as he carried the cross, or how Mary felt when she kissed Jesus's face when he was taken from the cross."

Julie later felt inspired to tuck a blessed Miraculous Medal under Ruth's pillow. It was one that I had sent her earlier along with her book order. Julie was aware that one of the special promises of the Miraculous Medal is the grace of a peaceful death. Very soon after, Ruth passed on peacefully in her sleep from this earthly life to her eternal reward.

POINTED IN THE RIGHT DIRECTION

In February of 2008 a woman named Malindia called me on the phone to talk with me about Mother Teresa. She was in the process of painting and decorating a room in honor of Mother Teresa at the Queen of Saints retreat house in Bridgeport, Connecticut. We had a nice chat about Mother Teresa, the spiritual giant we both admired, and after speaking with her I felt inspired to send her a Miraculous Medal, which was blessed by Pope Benedict XVI. I mailed it out to her the next day.

Malindia finished painting the Mother Teresa room two days later, which was the day the blessed medal arrived. She put the medal on, and just two hours later she learned that she would have to move. A house around the corner from where she was renting burned down to the ground. Since Malindia was living in the house until a need arose, she had to move out to make room for the temporarily homeless family from the burned house.

Malindia leased a moving truck and decided to return to her hometown in Michigan. It was a long journey from Connecticut, but she sincerely believed that the Blessed Mother would take care of her. She was convinced that the blessed Miraculous Medal she wore would be a channel of much grace for her. She counted on Mother Teresa's intercession as well.

"The moment I received the Miraculous Medal was a turning point in my life. My time in Michigan has been fruitful in various ways. I've reconnected with people from school, from my former work, and of course, my family. I have worn the Miraculous Medal since I put it on February 25, 2008."

The Miraculous Medal played an important role in Malindia's friend's life as well. Maureen worked in a hospital chaplaincy program. So, Malindia purchased a number of Miraculous Medals and sent them to Maureen so that Maureen could give them out to some of the patients at the Bridgeport hospital.

Maureen gave Miraculous Medals to some of the patients she encountered. The medals from Malindia and others that Maureen purchased came in handy for another purpose as well. One of the mothers in Maureen's son's class at school was battling cancer on and off for several years. Maureen described the mom, whose name was Mary, as "always very positive, active, and involved with her kids and the school. You would never know that she had cancer. She even made meals for other people that were sick!"

Then Mary's cancer grew aggressively worse, and she required another round of treatments. The moms in the class who knew her arranged for meals to be delivered to the family. Maureen suggested the women gather together to pray a weekly rosary for the ailing mom and that they all wear a Miraculous Medal, too. "I would see people wearing the medals on chains around their neck, and one mom wore it on a bracelet and she is Greek Orthodox!" Maureen recalled. Mary was unable to meet with the others but faithfully prayed in unity with them at the time they prayed the rosary. She wore a Miraculous Medal as did her husband and sister.

A few months later, Mary passed away peacefully. Maureen feels strongly that Mary is at peace and watching out for her husband and boys. "She was such a light and beautiful person!"

Disabled on the Street

On a trip to a special conference in Rome, I was blessed to bring along two of my daughters. When I was finished with the conference, I took to the streets to do some sightseeing and soak up the flavors of beautiful Rome. Rounding a corner of a charming street market, my daughter Mary-Catherine and I came upon a disabled woman sitting on a piece of cardboard near a dumpster. My heart instantly sank. I was saddened to see the woman's stiff legs stretched out in front of her, with crutches lying beside her and a large number of knobby bumps protruding from her sparse wisps of hair. I think they were tumors.

I was overcome with compassion for this stranger on the street. This was her life, but I wanted to scoop her up off the street and rescue her somehow. A tear was forming in my eye. My daughter could see I was distressed and asked me if I had a Miraculous Medal with me that I could give her. I didn't think I did, but I dug into my purse and pockets anyway. I took out a large Miraculous Medal set on a key chain that I forgot was in my pocket. It had been blessed by Pope Benedict at his general audience the day before.

I kissed it, reached out my hand, and offered it to the woman. She took it from me, kissed it, and placed it into her pocket. I spoke to her in English while making hand motions, trying to let her know that the pope had blessed the medal. She nodded as if she understood.

I was exceedingly moved by my encounter with this woman on the street. I felt overwhelmed with love for her. Tears were streaming down my face, and I was trying to wipe them away quickly so as not to cause some kind of a scene. But I guess I wasn't thinking about that when I gently picked up the woman's hands in mine and began kissing them all over. I could see that she had tears in her eyes, too. I'll never forget meeting this woman. She was to me "Jesus in the distressing disguise of the poorest of the poor," as Mother Teresa would say of the poor she helped.

Blessings Amid a Harrowing Journey

The woman seated to the right of me on the plane seemed to be about the age of one of my daughters. As soon as our plane took off, the young woman became distressed and began to hyperventilate. I completely understand the reason for her anxiety—the plane seemed like it was going to plummet to the ground as it dipped dramatically and then was shoved from side to side by the turbulence.

I reached out my right hand and touched her arm. She was a complete stranger, but she was in distress, and the mother in me reached out to comfort her. Her tense breathing changed momentarily to relieved sighs—that is, until the next bout of turbulence occurred.

"Here. Do you want to hold my rosary?" I asked her. She quickly took it from my hands and drew it straight to her heart, again sighing. I had another rosary, and knew I could finish praying my rosary using it. The poor soul, I thought. The flight had started off all wrong. Others around us could be heard making remarks about the flight and gasping loudly at times when the plane made sudden, unexpected movements.

Whenever I travel, I usually carry a few sacramentals from the Church with me, so I reached in my carry-on bag to find something else that I could offer to the worried young woman. I pulled out a blessed Miraculous Medal. It was one of the very special ones I owned. Mother Teresa had given it to me during one of my visits with her. I handed it to the woman. She drew it to her heart and then immediately put it on the long, fashionable chain she was wearing.

I told her that Mother Teresa had given it to me, and that I was now giving it to her. She seemed very comforted with the sacramentals of the rosary and Miraculous Medal. We chatted, and she told me her name was Federica. With every bump of the plane (and there were many significant ones along our journey), I reached over and stroked her arm. Then, after an exceedingly long flight from Rome, Italy, to the United States, Federica handed me back my rosary, gave me a huge, tight hug, and thanked me profusely for helping her with her fears and for the gift of the special Miraculous Medal. We also exchanged contact information, and Federica assured me that if I returned to Rome I was welcome to visit her.

Daughter's Miraculous Medal Miraculously Found

My friend Linda's daughter, Jen, was an avid soccer player when she was in high school. One day, while practicing with her team after school, she felt her Miraculous Medal and chain fall into the grass. She immediately started looking where she had thought it might have fallen. Her teammates stopped practicing, too, and helped Jen to search for her medal. Unfortunately, they couldn't find it.

Jen felt sad about losing her medal. She believed that she had become very close to the Blessed Mother because of her Miraculous Medal. Linda told Jen not to worry and that she might still find it while practicing that week, but if not, she would find her another and have it blessed. Even with her mother's encouraging words, Jen was still disappointed.

The following morning, while Jen was packing her soccer bag for her after-school practice, she called out to her mom to come into her room. Jen explained to her mom that when she was packing a pair of socks into one of the side pockets of her duffel bag, she saw that at the bottom of the pocket was her Miraculous Medal along with her chain! She was very excited and also very surprised. She couldn't figure out how it had gotten in her bag. All the team bags are always lined up behind the sidelines of the field when they are practicing. Jen did not see anyone go near her bag at the practice.

Both mom and daughter were very happily surprised to see the lost medal in her bag. "I told Jen that, apparently, this is something Mary does not want her to be without either, and she now has it back!" her mom recalled.

Bringing Back Memories

My friend Terri and her mother, Ann, were longtime members of my parish. I always enjoyed visiting with them after Mass and sometimes at Ann's home.

As Ann reached her eighties, she began to suffer with Alzheimer's disease and many other physical hardships and eventually had to move from her home into an extended-care facility. With the progression of the illness, her memory began to fail. Someone who had been so engaged with family and parish life was now plagued with having no memory of her friends or events of her past, which was sad for Terri and her family to see. Terri had always enjoyed singing songs together with her mom, but Ann had forgotten those, too.

At eighty-eight years old, Ann took a serious fall. When I heard about Ann's accident, I gave Terri a blessed Miraculous Medal to bring to her. Terri recalled, "As I placed the medal in her hands, I told her it was from Donna at church." Terri watched as her mother looked down at the medal and then up at Terri's face, with a puzzled expression "that she often had when I spoke about any of her friends. But as she looked at and held the Miraculous Medal in her hands, she repeated Donna's name."

Ann was still holding the Miraculous Medal in her hand when, suddenly, a big smile spread across her face. "Donna, with the children at church—how is her little girl?"

"I was astounded that Mom remembered," Terri said. "She had not seen Donna and her family for several years. By the grace of God, Mom had been given a memory that brought her happiness." What could be better than that? Terri shared, "Mom wore that Miraculous Medal every day and night. Every time she touched it, she would smile the most beautiful and peaceful smile."

Terri believes that the Blessed Mother, through her Miraculous Medal, brought much grace to her mother, who had always been very devoted to Mary. "In August of 2010, Mom went to be with the Lord. Now she is smiling down on her children and grandchildren—that beautiful, peaceful smile. Praise God!"

Our Lady of the Miraculous Medal Intercedes

A woman I know named Lisa shared a story with me about the first pregnancy of her daughter, Amanda. She began by telling me that Amanda's pregnancy went very well. Amanda not only nourished her pregnant body to nurture her unborn baby, but she fed her soul, too, by reading about Church teachings while she awaited childbirth.

"On December 12, Amanda went to her scheduled thirty-six-week check-up with her obstetrician, and it was suspected that her amniotic fluid might be low, thus posing a danger to the baby," Lisa said. An immediate ultrasound was ordered by the doctor in order to check on the baby and Amanda's uterus. Since the doctor's suspicion was confirmed, Amanda was admitted to the hospital and treated with IV fluids, "in hopes of raising her fluid level, and for monitoring of the baby, who was shown to be healthy and seemingly unaffected by the low fluid," continued Lisa.

Amanda remained in the hospital while the fluid level and health of the baby continued to be monitored. She was also under the care of a perinatologist who, along with her obstetrician, believed that to allow her to deliver on her January 5 due date could endanger the baby.

Amanda and Lisa both wore the blessed Miraculous Medals I sent them, and Lisa faithfully prayed the novena prayer and the prayer of devotion to the Miraculous Medal daily, beseeching Mary's intercession for a good outcome for Amanda and her baby. Amanda prayed as well. Sometimes she kissed her medal and clasped it in her hand, holding it to her heart when she prayed, being very cognizant that she was wearing a special, blessed sacramental that was directly linked to the Blessed Mother.

"For the next four days, Amanda's fluid level remained at a dangerously low level of five (a fluid level of four requires immediate delivery)," Lisa explained. The administering of the IV fluids did not help increase the amniotic fluid. Because of this, an induction date was scheduled for December 17, thus allowing Amanda to deliver at thirty-seven weeks.

Even though the scheduled date to deliver was three weeks earlier than Amanda's official due date, this timing is universally considered to be full term and safe to deliver the baby. However, Lisa and Amanda shared a concern that since the baby would be born early, he might be too small. The baby might therefore require neonatal intensive care until he was stronger and perhaps experience a tough start in life.

On December 16, an ultrasound technician checked Amanda's fluid one last time to be sure that the fluid had not dropped even further. "To everyone's surprise, the fluid had doubled to a level of ten!" Lisa shared. "The doctors were astonished because this drastic increase was seemingly impossible, but while the cause of the initial fluid drop remained uncertain, the doctors were still on schedule to induce her at thirty-seven weeks," Lisa explained.

A proud grandmother reported, "After a normal labor, Amanda delivered a healthy baby boy, whom she named Buck, weighing in at six pounds eight ounces, and he did not have to go to the NICU." Everyone was relieved and counted their blessings! "We were thankful for all of the prayers Amanda received during that time and for the blessed Miraculous Medals and prayers," Lisa said. Amanda added, "We will always remember that nothing is impossible with God and our Mother Mary."

Airplane Seatmate's Amazing Story

I zipped up my suitcase and was just about ready to head for the airport to film my television series for Catholic mothers at the EWTN network in Alabama. But first, I put a blessed Miraculous Medal in my pocket. If it would be God's will, I'd offer the medal to someone that day, I thought.

Unbeknownst to me, later on I would happen to sit down next to a woman who would openly share with me her traumatic and life-threatening ordeal. At first she was very quiet and sort of hid behind her magazine. Other than a quick hello as I plunked down in my seat, I refrained from entering into a conversation with the woman, since it appeared she desired a bit of privacy.

I settled in and quietly said my prayers. The pilot's voice came over the loudspeaker, telling us that because of favorable winds and weather conditions. We would arrive in Alabama about fifty minutes early.

"Was that fifty or fifteen?" my quiet seatmate asked me.

"It was actually fifty," I responded.

The ice was broken, and we started to converse. The lovely petite woman's name was Nancy. Somehow we got on the subject of faith and prayer. Maybe it was because I mentioned praying when flying; I really can't remember now. Because of how our conversation was flowing, I became very inspired to offer Nancy a blessed Miraculous Medal, reaching into my pocket for the one I placed there before I left Connecticut.

"You have no idea what this means to me," she told me as she reached behind her neck to unfasten her chain. What she did and said next gave me reason to pause and interiorly thank God. Nancy took her chain off her neck and placed the medal on it next to her cross. As she put the necklace back on her neck, she told me that she was a Methodist. I was rejoicing inside that she would accept the medal and even want to put it on.

Then, Nancy shared her remarkable story with me.

One morning while getting ready for work at her Alabama home, Nancy barely escaped with her life. While she was in the kitchen making her lunch, her back door flung wide open. In barged a crazed and violent man who immediately began pounding on her head.

Nancy was beside herself with shock and terrible pain from the merciless beating, but suddenly an inspiration flooded her brain. She blurted out to the intruder that she had some jewelry, hoping to distract him from hurting her further. He started pushing her toward her bedroom, and Nancy pointed to her jewelry box. That was when she discovered a way to escape and fled to her next-door neighbor's house.

The robber took off with the jewelry box as Nancy's neighbor fired away with his shotgun. The derelict dropped the jewelry box and was caught by the police and arrested. It turns out he was high on drugs at the time of his assault and attempted robbery.

As Nancy shared her shocking experience with me, she seemed calm and even happy to get it off her chest. She pulled her bangs aside to show me a scar on her forehead and pointed to the back of her head, where numerous sutures had been required to sew her head up after the brutal assault.

She explained that, by some miracle, she felt even closer to God after the attack occurred. In fact, she had been praying extra hard to God before it happened, which helped get her through this traumatic experience. After we chatted some more, I thanked her for sharing her story with me. I also told her that I was very thankful that God put us right near one another on the plane! I was thrilled that now Nancy was wearing a special blessed Miraculous Medal. O Mary, conceived without sin, pray for us who have recourse to thee!

A Miraculous Change of Events

My friend Alice was stricken with breast cancer. She felt very fortunate that a lumpectomy and chemotherapy treatments took care of ridding her body of cancer in time. Alice regained her strength and was relieved to finally let go of her fears. But one fateful day at a follow-up appointment, the doctor informed Alice that her cancer had returned and a mastectomy was required.

I sent Alice a get-well card with a blessed Miraculous Medal inside, hoping and praying that she would wear it. She wasn't Catholic, so I couldn't be sure that she would venture to put it on. But I was thrilled to learn later that she did indeed wear the medal. She wrote me a lovely thank-you card, stating that she was wearing the medal and informing me that all her cancer had vanished! Alice had followed up with additional medical appointments, and it was clearly determined that the cancer that was seen earlier was now completely gone. A mastectomy was not necessary. Alice was very pleased, relieved, and thankful.

He Gave Up His Seat and His Heart Was Transformed

When traveling back to Connecticut from Texas after my sister Barbara had died, I experienced a fascinating encounter on the plane. Just after takeoff, my heart went into one of its dreaded events. You see, I have a heart condition, which started over twenty-five years ago during a pregnancy. My heart races uncontrollably at times. The doctor tells me that it is electrical. When this happens, I am supposed to lie down and put my feet up in an attempt to get blood flowing to my heart so that my heart will return to the right rhythm.

I sat back in my seat a bit, relaxed, took a deep breath, and silently prayed. My heart continued to race. It would be a three-hour flight. If I didn't lie down, things would continue to get worse and I would end up in the hospital—if I even made it to the hospital on time.

I asked the flight attendant if there were any vacant seats that I could stretch out on—just for a few minutes. "We're totally full," she hastily blurted out without batting an eyelash. I asked if I could lie down in the aisle for a few minutes. It would be embarrassing to have to lie there while passengers stared at me, wondering what the heck I was doing, but I had no other choice but to lie on the dirty, narrow floor of the plane.

So, I folded up my jean jacket to tuck under my head as a makeshift pillow and got down on the floor. My heart kept on racing. I prayed, blessed myself with the Sign of the Cross, and prayed some more. The flight attendant came to me a couple minutes later and straight-out told me that I needed to move out of the way because she was about to bring the food cart through. I was already thoroughly humbled and embarrassed to be on the floor of the plane, and now I felt a bit hurt that the woman didn't seem to care and was making me move.

I stood up, dusted myself off, and was about to squeeze back into my middle seat, when my seatmate, the young man in the aisle seat, offered to move to the middle and allow me to sit on the aisle. The blend of feelings— embarrassment, exhaustion from the week before of caring for my sister and watching her die, sorrow over her death, extreme concern about my heart racing during my flight, the sting from the bluntness of the flight attendant, and then the gratitude for kindness shown to me by the man gifting me with his seat—caused me to shed a few tears and suddenly blurt out to him, "It's just that my sister just died—today!"

All of a sudden, my heart jumped back into the proper rhythm. I was thankful and relieved all at once. I told the young man, whose name was John, "Maybe I had to shed a few tears to help my heart." He was very quiet and simply looked at me. Then he wiped a tear from his eye and told me that he had gone to great pains to be certain that he would have an aisle seat on that flight, but after listening to me and learning what had just transpired in my life, he started to count his blessings and wanted to do something to help. He gave up his seat and was grateful for the chance to help another person rather than focus on his own wants.

I then felt I should offer John a blessed Miraculous Medal, which he was happy to receive. He immediately attached it to the chain he had under his clothing, which held his cross. My heart was so happy as I watched John put the blessed medal on his chain. He would be competing in a marathon in New York City the following day, and I promised him my prayers.

Spouses in Surgery and Transformed Hearts

I met a woman in the surgical waiting room at the hospital when my husband, Dave, was having an emergency surgery to remove his infected gall bladder. JoAn was also waiting for her husband, whose gall bladder was being removed, too. We got to chatting and ended up praying together for our husbands. I suddenly felt inspired to offer JoAn two blessed Miraculous Medals, one for her and one for her husband.

She told me that they both had been searching for a church to attend and that recently she had been praying often that God would direct her life. This was music to my ears. I was thankful that I could be even a tiny part of JoAn's faith journey. She happily accepted the medals. Later on, when John was discharged from the hospital, JoAn shared with me in an e-mail that she and John had purchased chains so that they could wear the blessed Miraculous Medals. She said that after they put them on she felt a strong tingling from the medal as she wore it. John slept peacefully each night while wearing his medal, although before that time he had nightmares each night ever since he had open-heart surgery several years before.

Soon after, JoAn informed me that she felt inspired to go back to church after meeting me and that she and her husband John would be joining a parish in their town very soon. And so they did.

JoAn told me over a year later that she feels increasingly close to the Blessed Mother each day and has begun to reach out to her in prayer regularly. She says that her prayers to Mary are really making a difference in her life, and she feels a tender relationship with Mother Mary unfolding. JoAn feels confident to invoke the Blessed Mother with her needs. This notion to pray to Jesus's Mother Mary is something very new to JoAn, who was raised a Protestant and was not taught about the active role that Mother Mary has in our lives. She values the Blessed Mother along with the medal and its role in her life and later asked me to send her a blessed Miraculous Medal for her sister, who would be undergoing surgery and chemotherapy.

Mother Mary to the Rescue

My seatmate and I began chatting on the flight home to Connecticut from Alabama. Our conversation turned to matters of faith and the Catholic Church. Joan expressed that she was trying to sort through a few problems she had with the Church. I took out a blessed Miraculous Medal and asked if I could give it to her. She was so happy to accept it. During the entire two-hour flight she held it tight in her hand as we chatted, occasionally looking at it. She told me she believed God had saved her life in a recent surgery and had a mission for her. She was trying to discern it. I recommended time with Jesus in the Blessed Sacrament to seek his answers and also the sacrament of confession to reap the benefits of transforming graces since she hadn't been in a while. Joan told me over and again that she felt it was meant to be that we sat near one another.

We decided to stay together a while longer at the next airport since we both had an hour before our connecting flights. When we began looking for a tram to ride to our distant gates, I spotted a young mother from our flight having a meltdown on the floor of the airport, crying, hysterical, and yelling at her two young children while frantically searching for something. I couldn't walk by. I got down on my knees to comfort her, asking if I could help. April was positive that her cell phone was still on the plane as she couldn't find it. Extremely upset, she had to use her inhaler. I suggested we call her phone with mine. She then heard it ringing through her luggage.

Joan appeared and began to help too. The mother in me asked April if I could give her a hug. She wholeheartedly accepted and squeezed me tight. She blurted out that both her mother and stepmother had abandoned her and she was going through a divorce and her fourteen-year-old sister was pregnant. I told her God was taking care of her. Her tears turned into sighs. I pulled out a blessed Miraculous Medal, touched it to mine, pointed to Mary on it and said, "Here, Mary is your Mother. Pray to her and ask her to help you mother your children." She lit right up, told me she was Catholic and took the medal (and my business card), sighing and thanking me. I promised my prayers.

I have no doubt that our Lord and his Mother Mary brought Joan, April, and I together. I am praying for April. Joan and I are in touch and will be getting together at a future talk I'm giving. I am in constant awe at how God works in our lives!

Passing on the Blessings

My friend Rosie in San Antonio, Texas, loves the Blessed Mother and prays often to Pope John Paul II and Mother Teresa for intercession for her family. So, you can imagine how happy she was when I gave her some blessed Miraculous Medals that I had placed on John Paul II's tomb and Mother Teresa's bed. "For me it was a beautiful, invaluable gift," she said. "I gave one to each in my family, my husband, my three sons, and my baby girl, Mariana. I've been wearing it since that day."

Rosie and her family pray the family rosary. "We always pray to Our Lady for protection and guidance. As our Mother promised, marvels of grace and health, peace and prosperity, have been shown to us. As Mary said, 'Those who wear it will receive great graces, especially if they wear it around the neck.'"

In addition, Rosie has a great devotion to the Miraculous Medal. She believes, "We have always the opportunity to help others with a word, a smile, our prayers, and the Miraculous Medal. It is simply an instrument to bring a person's prayers into focus and in submission to God's plan." Rosie asked me for additional blessed medals that she could give to others. She told me later about a few of the recipients of the blessed Miraculous Medals she offered.

"On one occasion a friend of mine called me to let me know that her husband was in the hospital in a serious condition," Rosie explained. "I went to visit them at the hospital and I brought a Miraculous Medal that you sent me." Rosie put in plain words to her friends the treasures of the medal, specifically "the Blessed Mother's protection in every circumstance of our lives." Rosie asked them to wear it and to pray to Our Lady.

"When my friend put the medal near her husband, I remember his face clearly. He was beaming with faith and full of hope that he would be out of the hospital and healed soon," Rosie told me. After a few days, he went home. He has been in excellent health, working and enjoying his family ever since.

Another time, one of Rosie's friends found out she was pregnant and was very upset. In fact, she started to cry when she shared the news with Rosie, since she was fearful of losing her job and of not having time for a baby. Rosie reassured her and told her that the baby was a blessing to her and her family.

When it was time for her friend to deliver her baby, Rosie visited her and brought one of the blessed Miraculous Medals. Her friend asked her to put the medal on her necklace. Her baby girl was born later that day, and the happy mom has never taken her blessed Miraculous Medal off. Rosie shared with me, "They are so crazy about her! The baby changed their lives."

Another time, Rosie sent a Miraculous Medal to two of her friends, a young couple who had two children and lived in another part of Texas. Rosie was very concerned for them because the father was in the hospital fighting for his life. He had never fully recovered from a heart-transplant surgery from five years before, and the family was always so sad that he was in the hospital so often. Rosie wrote a letter to go along with the blessed medal she sent, giving words of comfort and a promise of prayers for the family.

The family was very happy to receive the Miraculous Medal and felt a great deal of peace from it. About one month later, Rosie's friend died in complete peace. As Rosie recounted the story, she said, "Mary is part of our salvation, she is our Mother, and she brings her children through the sorrows of earth to the bliss of heaven."

Just as Rosie has requested blessed Miraculous Medals from me, so have others, and the blessings are being spread all around the world, as links in a chain stretching from Mary to Jesus.

The Tide Turned

My friend Louise told me she had misplaced the Miraculous Medal I gave her. She said, "I've been looking for it—I knew it was buried somewhere in the mess of my office. So, today, a repairman came to try and fix my phone and fax line, which has been out for three days."

The repairman seemed to be having trouble figuring out what was wrong. He told Louise she would need to replace her fax machine/printer. "I was moving things around so he could access the phone port, and I found my medal—to my great happiness! I quietly prayed with the medal that he would be able to resolve the problem."

The repairman poked around some more and confirmed that she needed to buy a new fax machine. But when he tried to hook her phone back up without the fax machine, the phone still didn't work. "More prayers and a little more rummaging on his part and he discovered that it was actually just a faulty phone cord, not my fax." Before the repairman left, everything was working again, and it ended up costing Louise nothing.

"I felt such peace when I prayed with that medal, and it was then that the tide turned. I have no doubt that this was a little Miraculous Medal intervention. I ended my day in peace and gratitude."

Gardening Blessings

One time when going out on an errand with my husband, I spotted our elderly neighbor pruning some of his bushes. My husband stopped the car so we could say hello. We chatted a little while, and Al, our neighbor, told us that he had not been feeling well lately. He's a cancer survivor and was now afflicted with shingles. I promised him my prayers and then pulled a blessed Miraculous Medal from my pocket and handed it to him. I told him that I had placed it on John Paul II's tomb and Teresa's bed. I knew he wasn't a churchgoer, but I felt inspired to give it to him. He seemed very appreciative to receive it. I leave the rest to Jesus and Mary.

Two Delivery Guys

Even when I am not out and about, the good Lord and his Blessed Mother give me many opportunities to evangelize and share the Miraculous Medal. One Ash Wednesday a deliveryman came to my door. I couldn't forget that detail, since the man had ashes on his forehead when he delivered my package. Since Lent was beginning, and I knew that the package was from one of my publishers and contained copies of a Lenten book I had written, I told the man that if he could wait just a minute, I could open the box and give him one. As I got the book out and signed it for him, he told me that his two grown children still go to Mass. So, I asked if he could wait one more minute, which he agreed to do, and then I ran up to my office and got four blessed Miraculous Medals, one for each of his family members.

Another time, a delivery truck pulled into my driveway to deliver my books a few days before I would be speaking to over two thousand women in Boston. It had begun to rain a bit earlier that day. When I looked out the window, I noticed the driver was already getting back into his truck after leaving ten boxes of my books in the middle of my driveway—in the rain! I quickly ran out and motioned to him to stop just as he was pulling away.

I told him that the boxes would be too heavy for me to bring in and pointed out that it was raining. The man explained that he was in a hurry and didn't have a hand truck with him to bring the boxes to the house. Since I had one in my garage, the kind man helped me get the books safely inside out of the rain. On the way to the door we chatted, and the man felt comfortable enough to open his shirt and show me a scar from a recent pacemaker insertion. He said he felt stressed, being just back on the job after time off for his surgery.

I told him I'd like to give him something. So, after going inside I gave him a couple of my books and also a blessed Miraculous Medal. This previously stressed-out man was now beaming and very relaxed. He thanked me immensely for the gifts and told me that this stop along his route was "totally meant to be!" He added, "And I never get this route!" I had no doubt that Jesus and Mary were working in this man's life that afternoon.

Grocery Store Encounter

I ran to the market to get a few items I'd need for dinner one Sunday after Mass and there bumped into good friends from my parish. Debbie told me that her husband Eric would be getting his thyroid surgically removed in about a week because he had thyroid cancer. Just then, Eric rounded the corner and dropped a few items into their cart. I asked him about his surgery, promised my prayers, and we chatted a few minutes. I found a blessed Miraculous Medal in my purse and handed it to him. He was very thankful to receive the medal but was more concerned about one of his students who recently lost her brother in a school shooting. He asked for a medal for her. Thankfully, I found one more medal, after much digging!

A couple of Sundays later when I walked into church I saw Eric standing at the back. When he saw me, he smiled and immediately opened his arms wide to embrace me. I went over to greet him and he thanked me for my prayers. He looked like the picture of health only a few days after his surgery. Eric told me he was doing great and that after the surgery he touched his Miraculous Medal to each of the nurses who had cared for him. He said they were very moved by his faithful gesture.

THE PHONE MAN

One day a phone truck pulled into my driveway. The technician walked up to my door and asked me if my phone service had been restored after the huge storm we had experienced a week earlier. I told him that the phone line was working fine now. There was no real reason for the phone man to be there. I hadn't called for him. But God had a reason—the man needed to tell me his story.

Dave began to tell me all about his near-death experience during the storm. The storm came on so suddenly that no one was prepared for it. The meteorologists didn't predict it. Dave was in the bucket of his truck, fixing phone wires, when the sky turned black. A sudden wind ruthlessly whipped up with great force. He immediately came down from the bucket. Lightning struck, with a deafening cracking sound. Dave jumped from where he was standing to the other side of the truck, where he dropped to the ground. A split second later, a tree came down in the exact spot where Dave had been standing. Catching his breath, Dave thanked God (whom he had not spoken to in a while) right then and there for saving his life.

We chatted some more. Then Dave, who less than ten minutes before had been a perfect stranger, asked me to pray for his son. I told him I would. I felt compelled to offer Dave two blessed Miraculous Medals. One was for him and one for his son. Dave was happy to accept them.

FAITHFUL IN CHINA

At a women's conference where I had given a speech, I met a woman who told me about her two-and-a-half-week trip to China to adopt her three-year-old daughter, Faith. Allison and her husband traveled to China and arrived in Wuhan from Beijing where they would meet little Faith for the first time. That morning, Allison woke up with a very painful eye. It was red and swollen and getting worse as time went on. She was nervous about seeing Chinese doctors since she didn't know the language but wanted to get better so she could meet Faith the following day.

"My thought was that I needed a miracle. I didn't have time nor did I feel comfortable seeing a doctor in China," she told me. "I just wanted to focus on being with my new daughter."

Allison believed in the power of prayer and the promised graces of the Miraculous Medal. She said, "I prayed, confident Mary would help me. I put the medal on my eye, prayed for intercession and a healing, and then prayed a Hail Mary. When I took the medal off my eye, it was healed!"

On the Way to Paris

My daughter Mary-Catherine was planning to study abroad in Paris during her junior year of college, which necessitated a trip to the French consulate in New York City. It was more than a two-hour drive to the city, so I prayed a rosary on the way, asking for help and grace during Mary-Catherine's appointment. We arrived at her appointment early and stood outside with a group of people who were also waiting for the doors to be opened. We could sense a bit of tension among the growing crowd. It is pretty much common knowledge that it's not an easy feat to obtain one's visa from the French Consulate, and this was the case for my son Joseph, who also studied in Paris—hence the nervous tension.

We would sometimes overhear an occasional nervous chuckle or a question uttered aloud to a fellow visa applicant. Once folks got over their initial case of nerves, they would ask questions like, "Did you remember 'such and such' document?" "How many times have you been here?" And we also heard commiserating stories about it being the second or third attempt for some of the folks to try to obtain a visa.

A twenty-something Jamaican woman named Darren, whose flight was leaving for Paris that very night, was pacing, anxiously wondering if she would be granted her visa. Her husband had left the day before, and she was to meet him for their honeymoon. My daughter and I became engaged in a lively conversation with Darren, which was good fun and also helped to kill some time.

I suppose because of something I said, Darren asked if I had a rosary with me. I told her I did and asked if she wanted to hold it. She was fidgety and seemed to have a lot of nervous energy. I pulled a rosary out of my purse and explained that Father John A. Hardon, S.J., a very holy priest I knew whom I considered to be a living saint, had blessed it. I hoped the blessed sacramental would help calm her and also inspire her. Darren was delighted to hold it for a while. I told her that I had prayed a rosary on the way to the appointment. I then pulled out a Miraculous Medal, touched it to the one I wear, since it was a gift to me from Mother Teresa, and told Darren that I had placed the medal on John Paul II's tomb and Teresa's bed. She could hardly believe I was gifting her with the medal, and a striking smile immediately spread across her face.

I thought I should give her a pamphlet about saying the rosary because I got the impression she wasn't familiar with the practice. I assured Darren that she didn't need to accept the gifts. I certainly didn't want to push them on her. "Are you kidding?" she asked. "I'm standing with a *Mary* (Mary-Catherine), I'm talking to her. I held a rosary. I received a medal. It's all meant to be!"

My heart was ecstatic, secretly rejoicing and thankful for Mother Mary's intercession. I gave Darren my business card in case she wanted to get in touch later on. We chatted the whole time until Mary-Catherine and Darren were called inside the consulate. And before we parted, I encouraged Darren to try her best to visit the chapel at Rue du Bac where Mary our Mother appeared to St. Catherine Labouré. After all, Darren would be in Paris!

Special Gifts of Devotion

Because Mary-Catherine (who was, by the way, named after the Blessed Mother Mary and St. Catherine of Labouré) spent a college semester in Paris, I became the very happy recipient of a blessed rosary chaplet and a rosary, which Mary-Catherine purchased for me at the gift shop at the chapel at Rue du Bac where the Blessed Mother had appeared to St. Catherine Labouré. She also had them blessed by the priest there.

I have carried that blessed rosary chaplet in my pocket every day since Mary-Catherine gave it to me. The rosary she gave me hangs in a special place at my home. On a trip to Texas to spend time with my sister Barbara when she was dying of leukemia, I kept my chaplet in my pocket and prayed with it at every opportunity. While in Texas, the cross somehow became detached from the chaplet, and until I could find a tool to fix it, I carried both pieces together in my pocket.

While there, I went out to lunch one day with my sister Alice Jean and her husband, Luis, one of the rare times I left Barbara's side. Later on that evening, I realized that the chaplet part was missing and I only had the cross in my pocket. I searched all over and sadly couldn't find the holy string of beads. I planned to call the restaurant and ask if they could look for it. But I never got the chance to call the restaurant because my sister's condition grew worse, and she was my priority and focus. God must have had his reasons for me having a broken chaplet, I figured, and then I turned my thoughts to Barbara alone.

A week later, when I was back in Connecticut, I thought about asking my sister Alice Jean if she would call the restaurant for me to see if they had found it. The chaplet was very special to me since Mary-Catherine had given it to me and also because of its origin. But I didn't need to ask my sister—when reaching into my purse for something, I pulled out the chaplet, which was at the bottom of my purse! I have no clue as to how it got there, but I was extremely thankful I had found it.

* * *

May Mother Mary embrace you with her motherly love and grant you many graces as well. Totus Tuus!

O Mary, conceived without sin, pray for us who have recourse to thee!

CHAPTER EIGHT

Devotion to Our Lady of the Miraculous Medal— Novenas and Prayers

Whenever I go to the chapel, I put myself in the presence of our good Lord, and I say to him, "Lord, I am here. Tell me what you would have me to do." If he gives me some task, I am content and I thank him. If he gives me nothing, I still thank him since I do not deserve to receive anything more than that. And then I tell God everything that is in my heart. I tell him about my pains and joys, and then I listen. If you listen, God will also speak to you, for with the good Lord, you have to both speak and listen. God always speaks to you when you approach him plainly and simply.[22]

—St. Catherine Labouré

MIRACULOUS MEDAL NOVENA

Opening Prayer

Come, Holy Spirit, fill the hearts of your faithful, and kindle in them the fire of your love.

Send forth your Spirit, and they shall be created; and you shall renew the face of the earth.

O God, you instructed the hearts of the faithful by the light of the Holy Spirit. Grant us in the same Spirit to be truly wise and ever to rejoice in his consolation, through Jesus Christ our Lord. Amen.

O Mary, conceived without sin, pray for us who have recourse to thee. (3 times.)

O Lord Jesus Christ, you have been pleased to glorify by numberless miracles the Blessed Virgin Mary, immaculate from the first moment of her conception. Grant that all who devoutly implore her protection on earth may eternally enjoy your presence in heaven, who, with the Father and the Holy Spirit, live and reign, God, forever and ever. Amen.

O Lord Jesus Christ, for the accomplishment of your works, you have chosen the weak things of the world, that no flesh may glory in your sight. And for a better and more widely diffused belief in the Immaculate Conception of your Mother, you have wished that the Miraculous Medal be manifested to St. Catherine Labouré. Grant, we beseech you, that filled with like humility, we may glorify this mystery by word and work. Amen.

Memorare

Remember, O most gracious Virgin Mary, that never was it known that anyone who fled to thy protection, implored thy help, or sought thy intercession was left unaided. Inspired by this confidence, I fly unto thee, O virgin of virgins, my Mother; to thee do I come, before thee I stand, sinful and sorrowful. O Mother of the Word Incarnate, despise not my petitions, but in thy mercy hear and answer me. Amen.

Novena Prayer

O Immaculate Virgin Mary, Mother of our Lord Jesus Christ and our Mother, penetrated with the most lively confidence in your all-powerful and never-failing intercession, manifested so often through the Miraculous Medal, we your loving and trustful children implore you to obtain for us the graces and favors we ask during this novena, if they be beneficial to our immortal souls, and the souls for which we pray: (Mention your request).

You know, Mary, how often our souls have been the sanctuaries of your Son who hates iniquity. Obtain for us then a deep hatred of sin and that purity of heart which will attach us to God alone so that our every thought, word, and deed may tend to his greater glory.

Obtain for us also a spirit of prayer and self-denial that we may recover by penance what we have lost by sin and at length attain to that blessed abode where you are the Queen of Angels and of People. Amen.

Act of Consecration to Our Lady of the Miraculous Medal

Virgin Mother of God, Mary Immaculate, we dedicate and consecrate ourselves to you under the title of Our Lady of the Miraculous Medal. May this medal be for each one of us a sure sign of your affection for us and a constant reminder of our duties toward you. Ever while wearing it, may we be blessed by your loving protection and preserved in the grace of your Son.

Most powerful Virgin, Mother of our Savior, keep us close to you every moment of our lives. Obtain for us, your children, the grace of a happy death, so that, in union with you, we may enjoy the blessing of heaven forever. Amen.

O Mary, conceived without sin, pray for us who have recourse to thee. (3 times.)[23]

LITANY OF LORETO

Lord, have mercy on us. *Lord, have mercy on us.*
Christ, have mercy on us. *Christ, have mercy on us.*
Lord, have mercy on us. *Lord, have mercy on us.*
Christ, hear us. *Christ, graciously hear us.*

God the Father of Heaven, *have mercy on us.*
God the Son, Redeemer of the world, *have mercy on us.*
God the Holy Ghost, *have mercy on us.*
Holy Trinity, one God, *have mercy on us.*
Holy Mary, *pray for us.*
Holy Mother of God, *pray for us.*
Holy Virgin of virgins, *pray for us.*
Mother of Christ, *pray for us.*
Mother of divine grace, *pray for us.*
Mother most pure, *pray for us.*
Mother most chaste, *pray for us.*
Mother inviolate, *pray for us.*

Mother undefiled, *pray for us.*

Mother most amiable, *pray for us.*

Mother most admirable, *pray for us.*

Mother of good counsel, *pray for us.*

Mother of our Creator, *pray for us.*

Mother of our Redeemer, *pray for us.*

Virgin most prudent, *pray for us.*

Virgin most venerable, *pray for us.*

Virgin most renowned, *pray for us.*

Virgin most powerful, *pray for us.*

Virgin most merciful, *pray for us.*

Virgin most faithful, *pray for us.*

Mirror of justice, *pray for us.*

Seat of wisdom, *pray for us.*

Cause of our joy, *pray for us.*

Spiritual vessel, *pray for us.*

Vessel of honor, *pray for us.*

Singular vessel of devotion, *pray for us.*

Mystical rose, *pray for us.*

Tower of David, *pray for us.*

Tower of ivory, *pray for us.*

House of gold, *pray for us.*

Ark of the covenant, *pray for us.*

Gate of Heaven, *pray for us.*

Morning Star, *pray for us.*

Health of the sick, *pray for us.*

Refuge of sinners, *pray for us.*

Comforter of the afflicted, *pray for us.*

Help of Christians, *pray for us.*

Queen of Angels, *pray for us.*

Queen of Patriarchs, *pray for us.*

Queen of Prophets, *pray for us.*

Queen of Apostles, *pray for us.*

Queen of Martyrs, *pray for us.*

Queen of Confessors, *pray for us.*

Queen of Virgins, *pray for us.*

Queen of all Saints, *pray for us.*

Queen conceived without original sin, *pray for us.*

Queen of the most holy rosary, *pray for us.*

Queen of peace, *pray for us.*

Lamb of God, who takes away the sins of the world, *spare us, O Lord.*

Lamb of God, who takes away the sins of the world, *graciously hear us, O Lord.*

Lamb of God, who takes away the sins of the world, *have mercy on us.*

Pray for us, most holy Mother of God, *that we may be made worthy of the promises of Christ.*

Let us pray:

O God, whose only begotten Son, by his life, death, and resurrection has purchased for us the rewards of eternal life, grant, we beseech you, that while meditating on the mysteries of the most holy rosary of the Blessed Virgin Mary, we may imitate what they contain and obtain what they promise, through Christ our Lord. Amen.

LITANY OF THE IMMACULATE HEART OF MARY

Lord, have mercy on us. *Lord, have mercy on us.*

Christ, have mercy on us. *Christ, have mercy on us.*

Lord, have mercy on us. *Lord, have mercy on us.*

Christ, hear us. *Christ, graciously hear us.*

God the Father of Heaven, *have mercy on us.*

God the Son, Redeemer of the world, *have mercy on us.*

God the Holy Spirit, Sanctifier of souls, *have mercy on us.*
Holy Trinity, one God, *have mercy on us.*

Heart of Mary, always immaculate, *pray for us.*
Heart of Mary, full of grace, *pray for us.*
Heart of Mary, blessed among all hearts, *pray for us.*
Heart of Mary, tabernacle of the Most Holy Trinity, *pray for us.*
Heart of Mary, most similar to the Heart of Jesus, *pray for us.*
Heart of Mary, object of indulgences of the Heart of Jesus, *pray for us.*
Heart of Mary, as beautiful as the lily among thorns, *pray for us.*
Heart of Mary, crowned with the roses of innocence, *pray for us.*
Heart of Mary, always hidden from the snares of the enemy, *pray for us.*
Heart of Mary, mediator between God and men, *pray for us.*
Heart of Mary, guarding the secrets of heaven, *pray for us.*
Heart of Mary, abyss of humility, *pray for us.*
Heart of Mary, throne of mercy, *pray for us.*
Heart of Mary, who loves the Father with a Daughter's love, *pray for us.*
Heart of Mary, united to the Son with a Mother's love, *pray for us.*
Heart of Mary, united to the Holy Spirit with a Spouse's love, *pray for us.*
Heart of Mary, ocean of goodness, *pray for us.*
Heart of Mary, miracle of innocence and purity, *pray for us.*
Heart of Mary, mirror of all divine perfection, *pray for us.*
Heart of Mary, where the Blood of Christ, the price of our redemption, was formed, *pray for us.*
Heart of Mary, whose desires sped up the salvation of the world, *pray for us.*
Heart of Mary, which obtained grace for sinners, *pray for us.*
Heart of Mary, which most faithfully keeps the words and actions of Jesus, *pray for us.*
Heart of Mary, pierced by the sword of sorrow, *pray for us.*
Heart of Mary, most afflicted by the Passion of Christ, *pray for us.*
Heart of Mary, nailed to the cross with Christ, *pray for us.*

Heart of Mary, buried by sorrow with Jesus in the tomb, *pray for us.*

Heart of Mary, enlivened by joy in the Resurrection, *pray for us.*

Heart of Mary, full of sweetness in the Ascension of Jesus, *pray for us.*

Heart of Mary, crowned with the new fullness of grace coming from the Holy Spirit, *pray for us.*

Heart of Mary, consolation of the afflicted, *pray for us.*

Heart of Mary, refuge of sinners, *pray for us.*

Heart of Mary, hope and sweet aid of those who love you, *pray for us.*

Heart of Mary, help of the dying, *pray for us.*

Heart of Mary, joy of all saints, *pray for us.*

Lamb of God, who takes away the sins of the world, *forgive us, Lord.*

Lamb of God, who takes away the sins of the world, *hear us, Lord.*

Lamb of God, who takes away the sins of the world, *have mercy on us.*

Jesus Christ, hear us. *Jesus Christ, graciously hear us.*

Pray for us, Immaculate Heart of Mary, *that we may be worthy of obtaining the promises of Christ.*

Let us pray:

God of goodness, you filled the most holy and Immaculate Heart of Mary with feelings of mercy and kindness, which fill the Heart of Jesus Christ, your Son. Grant to all those who honor this virginal Heart the grace to keep until death in perfect harmony with the feelings and inclinations of the Sacred Heart of Jesus Christ, who lives and reigns with you and the Holy Spirit forever and ever. Amen.

PRAYER OF CARDINAL JOHN HENRY NEWMAN

Lord, have mercy. *Lord, have mercy.*

Christ, have mercy. *Christ, have mercy.*

Lord, have mercy on us. *Lord, have mercy on us.*

Christ, hear us. *Christ, graciously hear us.*

God the Father of Heaven, *have mercy on us.*
God the Son, Redeemer of the world, *have mercy on us.*
God the Holy Spirit, *have mercy on us.*
Holy Trinity, one God, *have mercy on us.*

Heart of Mary, *pray for us.*
Heart of Mary, after God's own Heart, *pray for us.*
Heart of Mary, in union with the Heart of Jesus, *pray for us.*
Heart of Mary, the vessel of the Holy Spirit, *pray for us.*
Heart of Mary, shrine of the Trinity, *pray for us.*
Heart of Mary, home of the Word, *pray for us.*
Heart of Mary, immaculate in your creation, *pray for us.*
Heart of Mary, flooded with grace, *pray for us.*
Heart of Mary, blessed of all hearts, *pray for us.*
Heart of Mary, Throne of glory, *pray for us.*
Heart of Mary, Abyss of humbleness, *pray for us.*
Heart of Mary, Victim of love, *pray for us.*
Heart of Mary, nailed to the cross, *pray for us.*
Heart of Mary, comfort of the sad, *pray for us.*
Heart of Mary, refuge of the sinner, *pray for us.*
Heart of Mary, hope of the dying, *pray for us.*
Heart of Mary, seat of mercy, *pray for us.*

Lamb of God, who takes away the sins of the world, *spare us, O Lord.*
Lamb of God, who takes away the sins of the world, *graciously hear us, O Lord.*
Lamb of God, who takes away the sins of the world, *have mercy on us.*

Immaculate Mary, meek and humble of heart, *conform our hearts to the heart of Jesus.*

Let us pray:

O most merciful God, who for the salvation of sinners and the refuge of the wretched has made the Immaculate Heart of Mary most like in tenderness and pity to the Heart of Jesus, grant that we, who now commemorate her most sweet and loving heart, may by her merits and intercession ever live in the fellowship of the Hearts of both Mother and Son, through the same Christ our Lord. Amen.

[A C K N O W L E D G M E N T S]

I WOULD LIKE TO EXPRESS my gratitude to all who have guided me, prayed for me, and loved me throughout my life, including my family and friends, especially my parents, Eugene Joseph and Alexandra Mary Uzwiak Cooper, and my brothers and sisters: Alice Jean, Gene, Gary, Barbara, Tim, Michael, and David. I offer thanks to my friend and spiritual guide, Father Bill C. Smith, for his love and continual guidance from heaven, as well as to my friend, spiritual guide, and my daughter's godfather, Servant of God Father John A. Hardon, S.J., for his marvelous wisdom and continued prayers and guidance from heaven. I am eternally indebted to all.

I would also like to thank my grandmother Alexandra Theresa Karasiewicz Uzwiak for her inexhaustible love, guidance, and inspiration; my godmother, Aunt Bertha Uzwiak Barosky, for her love and contagious optimism; and my "other mother," my friend and mentor, dear Mother Teresa, for her selfless lessons of love imparted to me and for her continued guidance and prayers from heaven. I am grateful, of course, as well to dear Blessed Mother Mary for mothering me, protecting me, and giving me and many others the gift of the Miraculous Medal!

My children have always been my utmost vocation in life. Words can never express my love for you, Justin, Chaldea, Jessica, Joseph, and Mary-Catherine!

My husband, David, the wind beneath my wings, thank you for your love and support!

This book wouldn't be possible without the publisher. My heartfelt thanks goes out to Claudia Volkman, Louise Pare, Father Dan Kroger, O.F.M., and the wonderful team at Servant Books for their partnership in getting this book out to you.

Lastly, with my deepest gratitude, my loving prayers go out to all who are connected with me through my books and talks. God bless you all! O Mary, conceived without sin, pray for us who have recourse to thee!

[R E S O U R C E S]

THE BLESSED MOTHER EXPRESSED THROUGH her apparitions her desire for all her children to wear the Miraculous Medal. St. Pius X established the Association of the Miraculous Medal to fulfill her wishes.

The association of the faithful of the Miraculous Medal (called the Miraculous Medal Association or Association of the Miraculous Medal) which St. Pius X established is composed of laity, clergy, and members of institutes of the consecrated life and societies of apostolic life who wear the Miraculous Medal and honor it with a Christian and apostolic life. It was approved and recognized by the Church by His Holiness St. Pius X, through the *Dilectus filius* on July 8, 1909, which placed it under the direction of the superior general of the Congregation of the Mission and the Company of the Daughters of Charity. The statutes were revised and approved on April 14, 2010, by the Vatican Congregation for Institutes of Consecrated Life and Societies of Apostolic Life. According to the statutes, the association's purpose is "to render due honor to Mary Immaculate, first by sanctifying ourselves, and second by contributing to the sanctification of our neighbor by means of this medal."

Indulgences have been attached to wearing the Miraculous Medal as an encouragement for people to become members. Those who are conferred the Miraculous Medal by a priest may gain a plenary indulgence (under the usual conditions of confession, Holy Communion, and prayer for the intention of the pope) on the following days: the day of investiture; the anniversary of the establishment of the association, July 8; and these feasts: the Queenship of Mary, August 22; St. Vincent de Paul, September 27; the Manifestation of the Miraculous Medal, November 27; and St. Catherine Labouré, November 28. These indulgences are applicable to the souls in purgatory. Two conditions must be fulfilled, however, to share in these indulgences. First, the person must be invested in the Miraculous Medal by a priest according to the official rite, and second, he or she must wear the medal hanging from the neck on the breast.

There are no obligations as a member of the association. But members are urged to pray often the prayer on the Miraculous Medal, "O Mary, conceived without sin, pray for us who have recourse to thee."

The religious and devotional international center for the Miraculous Medal is located at the Chapel of Our Lady of the Miraculous Medal, 140 Rue du Bac, 75340 Paris, Codex 07, France. The canonical center is the place of residence of the director general: Casa Generalizia, Via dei Capasso 30, 00164 Rome, Italy.

DAUGHTERS OF CHARITY

Compagnie de Filles de la Charité

140 Rue du Bac

75340 Paris Cedex 07

France

Website of the Daughters of Charity of St. Vincent de Paul and the international website of the Miraculous Medal: http://www.parisdigest.com/paris_information.php?parisdigest_source=http://www.parisdigest.com/monument/Chapelle-de-la-medaille-miraculeuse.htm&url=http://filles-de-la-charite.org/home

Information on becoming a Daughter of Charity: http://www.daughters-of-charity.org/exploring/steps_becoming_a_daughter.html

THE CENTRAL ASSOCIATION OF THE MIRACULOUS MEDAL

The Central Association of the Miraculous Medal was started in 1915 to spread devotion to Mary Immaculate through her Miraculous Medal. It also helps young men to become priests, aids infirm priests, and assists the poor.

475 East Chelten Avenue

Philadelphia, Pennsylvania 19144

Toll Free: 1-800-523-3674

Website: http://www.cammonline.org or www.MiraculousMedal.org

Association of the Miraculous Medal

The Association of the Miraculous Medal was established in 1918 in Perryville, Missouri, by the Western Province of the Congregation of the Mission in the United States. It was initially operated by the Saint Mary's Seminary students under the direction of their religious superior. Later on, the association expanded and was given its own director and staff.

1811 West Saint Joseph Street

Perryville, Missouri 63775

Website: http://www.amm.org/

Archconfraternity of Notre-Dame-des-Victories

The center of the devotion for the archconfraternity of Notre-Dame-des-Victories (started by Father Desgenette) in the United States is the Basilica of Our Lady of Victory, 767 Ridge Road, Lackawanna, New York.

[N O T E S]

1. Jill Haak Adels, *The Wisdom of the Saints: An Anthology* (New York: Oxford University Press, 1989), p. 130.
2. Father Joseph Dirvin, *St. Catherine of the Miraculous Medal* (Charlotte, N.C.: St. Benedict and Tan, 1981).
3. Dirvin, *St. Catherine of the Miraculous Medal.* Available at http://www. ewtn.com/library/MARY/CATLABOU.htm. All the references to the Blessed Virgin's appearances to St. Catherine have been taken from this source.
4. Dirvin, *St. Catherine of the Miraculous Medal.*
5. M. Aladel, C. M., H.L., *The Miraculous Medal: Its Origin, History, Circulation, Results* (Philadelphia: Kilner & Co., 1880), p. 6.
6. Dirvin, *St. Catherine of the Miraculous Medal.*
7. Constitutions of the Daughters of Charity, c.2.16.
8. Constitutions of the Daughters of Charity, c.2.16.
9. Elizabeth Charpy, D.C., *A Way to Holiness: Louise de Marillac* (Dublin: Mount Salus, 1990).
10. Charpy, *A Way to Holiness.*
11. Available at http://www.daughters-of-charity.org.
12. Daughters of Charity of St. Vincent de Paul West Central Province, http://www.daughters-of-charity.org.
13. Aladel, *The Miraculous Medal,* p. 10.
14. Aladel, *The Miraculous Medal.*
15. Dirvin, *St. Catherine of the Miraculous Medal.*
16. Dirvin, *St. Catherine of the Miraculous Medal.*
17. Aladel, *The Miraculous Medal.*
18. Aladel, *The Miraculous Medal,* p. 39.

19. Aladel, *The Miraculous Medal,* p. 238.

20. Dirvin, *St. Catherine of the Miraculous Medal.*

21. Pope Pius XII on St. Catherine Labouré's canonization ceremony, July 27, 1947.

22. Sarah Gallick, *The Big Book of Women Saints* (New York: Harper Collins, 2009), p. 358.

23. These prayers are commonly known as prayers of the Miraculous Medal or of St. Catherine Labouré. This Miraculous Medal novena from opening prayer to here can be found in many books and at http://www.communityofhopeinc.org/Prayer%20Pages/Saints/catherine%20laboure.html.

About the Author

Donna-Marie Cooper O'Boyle is a Catholic wife and mother of five children and host and creator of EWTN's TV series *Everyday Blessings for Catholic Moms* and *Catholic Mom's Café*. She was privileged to know Blessed Mother Teresa of Calcutta personally over a ten-year period. She's been a catechist for over twenty-five years, an internationally known speaker, an award-winning journalist, and a bestselling author of numerous Catholic books including *The Domestic Church: Room by Room* and *Embracing Motherhood*. Donna-Marie's work can also be found in several magazines and publications, on the Web, and on her many blogs.

Contact Donna-Marie for speaking events at DMCOBoyle@aol.com and about her Catholic pilgrimages at Donnamariepilgrimages@gmail.com. Learn more at www.donnacooperoboyle.com.